RUMORS

MW01173968

For you were once darkness, but now you are light in the Lord. Walk as children of light (for the fruit of the Spirit is in all goodness, righteousness, and truth), finding out what is acceptable to the Lord. And have no fellowship with the unfruitful works of darkness, but rather expose them. For it is shameful even to speak of those things which are done by them in secret. But all things that are exposed are made manifest by the light, for whatever makes manifest is light. Therefore He says: "Awake, you who sleep, Arise from the dead, And Christ will give you light." Eph 5:8-14 NKJV

TABLE OF CONTENTS

Preface

Introduction

CHAPTER 7) pg.169
A THOUSAND YEARS OF CHANGE

Note: to the reader.
I've updated this work from 2018. The substance is the same, but I never edited the original manuscript. It has now been formatted for a better reading experience. I've updated the Preface, Intro, and Summaries for North & South. I have also made two corrections:
1: The people did not elect EU President Jean Claude Juncker; the EU parliament also appointed him.
2: Speculation typo changed.
" *I met to say…* "I don't believe the southern alliance can become strong starting confrontations with superpowers in their infancy."
I've also moved tools of interpretation to the chapters they apply.

PREFACE.

I've always wanted to sit down and review the many passages that speak about the key players of the last day's events. It was essential to identify the players on all sides and place them in the order of battle. I knew doing this would give me a more apparent worldview of what was happening around me. It has done just that.

Believers in the scriptures have a perspective the greatest geopolitical tacticians and think tanks don't have. God, through the scriptures, has revealed to us what is to come. Before the early 1900s, no one could conceive the restoration of Israel. The land, people, and language were lost for centuries. The scriptures said it would happen. It happened. If you looked at the political landscape, you could see the pieces forming. It began in 1881 when a large group of Jewish immigrants, over 25,000, began purchasing land and building settlements in Palestine. The Ottoman Turks controlled this territory. How probable was the Jewish nation in the middle of an Islamic empire? When this story hit the newsstands around the world, every bible student understood the significance. A generation later, it happened nationhood. The Bible has a lot to say about the nations and battles of the last days. If we believe what God says, the conclusions will be that we will have eyes to see where today's conflicts are heading.

An excellent example of this is the rarely reported conflicts in the Mediterranean Sea. We often focus on the Persian Gulf, but the Bible speaks of two major alliances of the last days known as the king of the North and South. It lists these nations in the Book of Ezekiel, and we see those allies forming before our eyes. The ongoing conflict between Turkey and Greece is forging alliances.

The previous immigration crises in Europe, some believe would lead to the Islamization of Europe. Just the opposite is true. What is happening today is a mere catalyst for its fragmentation and reshaping into what the word of God says it will become. This event has sparked movements that are driving nationalistic reforms. It's also driving the people from secularism to their European religious roots. (Rev 17:3-6) What's happening is beyond globalism; it's the formation and solidification of end-time alliances. We find most of this truth in the Book of Daniel. Jesus said in Matthew chapter twenty-four, there would be wars and rumors of wars. In the Book of Daniel, we see the key players of these wars.

Rumor of Wars is a book concerning the scriptural battles and confrontation leading to the war of all wars Armageddon. It identifies the national alliances written in the Bible that are forming before our eyes or will begin soon. It speaks of the destiny of crucial nations like Turkey, Europe, Egypt, Israel, the United States, and many more. Rumor of Wars is a look from a biblical perspective at what is coming.

INTRODUCTION.

My goal in this book is to set out the players and scenarios from the book of Daniel, Revelation, and other scriptures to portray a picture of the end time conflicts. Embarking upon this journey is more than I could have imagined. You can see these events unfolding on the world stage today almost faster than I can write about them. In the second half of this book, I go through each conflict. What I didn't foresee is the journey that I would have to travel to identify and discover these players. It's a journey I hope every reader will take with me. Understanding the phenomenal prophecies God has given us comes with requirements, the biblical test of interpretation. This is the standard I would like to challenge all who seek the mysteries of the scriptures.

When you check out books or visit various sites concerning the last days and end time prophecy the number of videos, articles, and information are overwhelming. I found some good well studied and thought-out information. This, unfortunately, was the exception. I also had to navigate a field of land mines. Land mines of error, falsehood, and deception. Declarations that pop stars and politicians are the coming beast because of some mythical calculations. Others state the mark of the beast is related to a day of the week and a multitude of theories that can stand without biblical support. That's right; they didn't need the bible to prove their point. It reminded me of Nebraska Man, one of the missing links of humanities evolution from ape to man, discovered by geologist Harold Cook in 1917. The problem is the only fossil found was a tooth. So, they built a whole ape man from a tooth. No other supporting evidence. They made pictures; they gave lectures; they wrote books and articles on the great ape man discovery, Nebraska Man. They later found the tooth belonged to an ape. I have placed some basic rules for interpretation in the beginning of most chapters.

I believe these truths will illuminate my reasoning's and conclusions.

The truth, information, and revelation I received during the writing of this commentary at points seemed overwhelming. I've attempted to keep it as simple as possible, but I must warn you. These passages are so tightly interconnected that it's almost impossible to recognize one truth without understanding how the others are connected. These are the deep waters for those who know Christ and desire to dive deeper into the waters of God's word. This book is about 170 pages. Please take your time and use your Bible to follow and fact check. You will need it. Happy treasure hunting.

CHAPTER 1)

OUR JOURNEY BEGINS: DANIEL CH 10.

Interpreting tool

Context: Identifying the beginning or end of a thought or season of time. It's also understanding the history or culture, the truth is found and recognizing the **literal or figurative usages of a word or text**. Jesus dealing with the issue of divorce gave them historical and cultural context. They had the law. Jesus gave them the context on why the law was written, revealing their incorrect use of the law. Understanding context led me to a hidden truth in the life of Daniel. Daniel's unusual fast in Daniel Chapter 10 resulted from a cultural obstacle he had to face. One placed there by God.

FINDING THE PATH

God has revealed to us, especially in the book of Daniel, the final players of the end-time conflicts.

If we believe we're living in the last days, then we must also think that the present geopolitical players on the world's stage will eventually be funneled into the scenarios found in the scriptures. What we see happening today is the molding of the conflicts and alliances to come. This is the path we find in Daniel.

Three of the most challenging chapters of Daniel's books are the final three, ten through twelve.

In these chapters, Daniel takes us from the Persian rule to anti-Christ and then to the end of the age. Before we interpret what's been written, we must first understand how this book is laid out.

I heard it said that the book of Daniel is not in order. The book is very orderly. The truth is its order is not chronological. The twelve books are divided in half. Chapter one through six is a chronological record of Daniel's time in Babylon and Persia under Darius and King Cyrus. It records him being taken from Israel in his youth. It speaks of the challenges, tests, and victories of living through the reigns of many great Kings and his service to them.

Chapter seven through twelve is different altogether. Daniel is recounting personal visions and revelations. Chapter seven is the four great beasts. Chapter eight is the vision of the goat and ram. Chapter nine is the revelation on the seventy weeks. Chapters 10 through 12 are the greatest of all. They reveal the wonders of the final conflict at the end of the age.

UNDERSTANDING THE VISION

Dan 10:1 In the third year of Cyrus king of Persia a thing was revealed unto Daniel, whose name was called Belteshazzar; and the thing was true, but the time appointed was long: and he understood the thing, and had an understanding of the vision. Dan 10:2 In those days...

The reference Daniel uses in the next verse is, "In those days."

Daniel is about to explain how he came to the conclusions in the previous verse. Daniel states, the message was valid, but the appointed time was long; and he understood the message and understood the vision. In verse one, Daniel, in a moment, sums up everything he is about to reveal. Daniel says first, "it's true." We must understand Daniel's been given this vision at the end of his life. This is his last vision. He can now see critical players stepping upon the stage of prophecy, validating what had already been revealed and what he is about to demonstrate to the reader. Daniel also understood that the fulfillment of this prophecy would not come for many generations.

Dan 12:4 But thou, O Daniel, shut up the words, and seal the book, even to the time of the end:

That's why the angel also says...

Dan 12:13 "But you, go your way till the end; for you shall rest, and will arise to your inheritance at the end of the days." The beauty of the resurrection!

The third year of King Cyrus refers to the third year after his conquest of Babylon, which included Judea. Cyrus was one of the greatest Persian kings. Known as Cyrus II, he became the greatest conquer of his time, and his fidelity to those he conquered earned him the title Cyrus the Great. Cyrus conquered Babylon in 538 BC. His third year would have been 535 BC. What's confused many readers is the reference to King Darius seems to put him in the same period as King Cyrus. Even Daniel says, Dan 6:28 So this Daniel prospered in the reign of Darius, and the reign of Cyrus, the Persian.

This is not a typo nor an error. History records that King Darius the Great of Persia reigned 16 years later after the death of Cyrus the Great.

Yet Daniel places the name of Darius before Cyrus in his recollection. It's important to remember that Daniel's first revelation of this great power that would replace Babylon was: Dan 8:20 The ram which thou sawest having two horns are the kings of Media and Persia. Eventually, the kingdom became just the Persian Empire, but that was not its start. The Darius that Daniel speaks of is not Darius the Great but Darius the Meade. When Cyrus conquered Babylon in 538BC, history states Nabonidus was its king. His oldest son was named Belshazzar. The General that took Babylon was Ugbaru, also known as Darius the Meade.

Dan 11:1 Also I in the first year of Darius the Mede, even I, stood to confirm and to strengthen him:2 And now will I show thee the truth.

The angel revealed to Daniel that from the start of his fast, he was heard. We can learn much from this. It was not a typical fast, and that's because this was not a typical time. It was not a fast designed by Daniel for longevity, but of necessity. Daniel began his fast on the third day of the first month of the year. Most commentators agree this is the month of Nisan. (The Persians, Babylonians, and Hebrew Calendars began in March) The angel's answer came on the twenty-fourth day. Minus three full weeks brings us to the third day of the month of Nisan. It was the first month for both Babylonian and Hebrew calendars. The month the Passover, as well as the Feast of Unleavened Bread, was to be observed. Daniel was so driven for answers that he disregarded the ordinance of the Passover. Daniel was so desperate for answers from God that he didn't wait for the ending of the feasts. He fasted during them.

This would explain Dan 10:3 ...I ate no pleasant food, no meat or wine came into my mouth, nor did I anoint myself at all, till three whole weeks were fulfilled.

This reveals early on that we don't serve a God of legalism. Daniels's love and passion gave him focus. He recognized the urgency of his time. His Faith in an all-knowing God who hears and answers his children is what drove him. He received more than he could ever imagine.

The story begins with a vision unlike any Daniel has received until this time. A Revelation of Jesus Christ.

Dan 10:5 Then I lifted up mine eyes, and looked, and behold a certain man clothed in linen, whose loins were girded with fine gold of Uphaz:6 His body also was like the beryl, and his face as the appearance of lightning, and his eyes as lamps of fire, and his arms and his feet like in color to polished brass, and the voice of his words like the voice of a multitude.

This is not just any revelation of Christ. It's Christ the warrior, The Lord of Host, as shown in Revelation chapters 1 & 19, where the sword of His mouth comes forth and his garments stained with blood. Metals have meaning in the scriptures. Brass or bronze is a symbol of sacrificial judgment that tends toward redemption, as iron is a symbol of judgment that tends toward wrath. Daniel's revelation concerns war and God's divine judgment. The vision that Daniel's receiving is Christ before the final battle, the judgment upon the nations.

2 Th 2:8 And then shall that Wicked be revealed, whom the Lord shall consume with the **spirit of his mouth, and** shall destroy with the brightness of his coming:

Daniel will learn the ultimate answers to his prayers, the deliverance of his people, and the fulfillment of prophecy concerning them and all humanity. The very presence of Christ in this vision laid Daniel prostrate. God chose this vision, this imagery, to reveal Himself to Daniel. Before ever showing him what was to come and granting him an understanding of what he had seen. God chose to begin here with the revelation that The Lord is a warrior! He truly is the Almighty. Today we, through the blood of the cross, understand the redemption of God. We are overwhelmed with the greatness of His Love. We often find ourselves surrounded by His companionate mercies. But before God unfolds the battles and atrocities that lead to the latter days.

Before God reveals wars that will be so fierce and awesome, the planet will be destroyed. The Heavenly Father gives Daniel a revelation of a side of Himself that His people often forget. He is a God of War.

Psa 24:8 **Who is this King of glory? The LORD strong and mighty, the LORD mighty in battle....:10 Who is this King of glory? The LORD of hosts,** he is the king of glory. Selah.

The Lord of Host means the Lord of all battle and War. The Lord of both spiritual and physical.

Paul said...2 Cor 10:4 (For the weapons of our warfare are not carnal, but mighty through God to the pulling down of strongholds;):5 Casting down imaginations, and every high thing that exalteth itself against the knowledge of God, and bringing into captivity every thought to the obedience of Christ;):6 And having in a readiness to revenge all disobedience when your obedience is fulfilled.

We see physical warfare throughout scripture.
David said...

2 Sam 22:35 He teacheth my hands to war; so that a bow of steel is broken by mine arms. Psa 144:1 ... Blessed be the LORD my strength, which teacheth my hands to war, and my fingers to fight:

NKJV: 2 Ki 19:35 And it came to pass on a certain night that the angel of the LORD went out, and killed in the camp of the Assyrians one hundred and eighty-five thousand; and when people arose early in the morning, there were the corpses; all dead.

Isa 13:5 They come from a far country, from the end of heaven, even the LORD, and the weapons of his indignation, to destroy the whole land.:6 Howl ye; for the day of the LORD is at hand; it shall come as a destruction from the Almighty.

When all things are said and done, our God has the power to fulfill His Promises to His People. God can break the reign of evil and deliver all those who trust in Him.

God plants this vision in the spirit of Daniel before he grants him the understanding we are about to pursue in chapters 10 through 12. God wants His people to understand that His word will reign through all difficulties and the hardest of times.

THE ANGEL

At this point, the vision has ended, an angel appears and lifts him. Daniel in v16 makes it clear **this encounter with the angel is separate from the vision.** It's important to recognize this separation.

Dan 10:16 Then, one who looked **like a man** touched my lips, and I opened my mouth and began to speak. I said to the one standing before me, "I am overcome with anguish **because of the vision**, my Lord, and I am helpless.

Failure to recognizing this has caused some to believe the demonic force from Persia could somehow resist the King of Kings or that the revelation of Daniel's vision and that of Johns in revelation (chapter 1:13-16) is not the same, shedding doubt on the consistency of scripture. The angel strengthens Daniel to receive the message. Then He gives Daniel a profound revelation.

Dan 10:12 Then said he unto me, Fear not, Daniel: for from the first day that thou didst set thine heart to understand, and to chasten thyself before thy God, thy words were heard, and I am come for thy words.:13 But the prince of the kingdom of Persia withstood me one and twenty days: but, lo, Michael, one of the chief princes, came to help me; and I remained there with the kings of Persia.

Throughout the scriptures, we see the destiny of cities and nations connected with the spiritually unseen powers affecting them. God spoke these words concerning Nebuchadnezzar after the judgment of insanity was pronounced upon him. Dan 4:26 .., after that **thou shalt have known that the heavens do rule**. Here is a revelation, God rules in the kingdom of men. He gives us free will, but our rise and fall will play into his ultimate plan of judgment and redemption.

Revelation Chapter 16:13 shows demonic spiritual activity that draws the nations' kings into the final war of wars, Armageddon. This clearly shows us that what's happening spiritually in a nation's leadership affects its direction.

Eph 6:12 For our struggle is not against flesh and blood, but against the rulers, against the authorities, against the powers of this dark world, and against the spiritual forces of evil in the heavenly realms.

CHAPTER 2)

THE IDENTITY OF THE SOUTHERN KINGDOM AND ITS ALLIES.

Interpreting tool

Ideas must be biblically based. The Bible is not interpreted as abstract ideas, which means visualized ideas with no scriptural evidence. You may believe you're led by the spirit but know the spirit works hand in hand with the scriptures. There should be a biblical base for your reasoning.

2 Pet 1:19-20: We have also a more <u>sure word</u> of prophecy; whereunto ye do well that ye take heed, as unto a light that shineth in a dark place, until the day dawn, and the day star arise in your hearts:20 Knowing this first<u>, that no prophecy of the scripture is of any private interpretation.</u> :21 For the prophecy came not in old time by the will of man: but holy men of God spake as they were moved by the Holy Ghost.

The scriptures must be your primary support. Secular history is good, the Bible is history, but historical accounts can be manipulated. Be careful of your source and **use history to join Biblical truths, not make a point**. Those truths should complement other truths in the scripture. "Mat 22:29 Jesus answered and said unto them, Ye do err, not knowing the scriptures, nor the power of God." Jesus referenced scripture. If we can build a doctrine or belief without scriptural support, we're building on shifting sand.

This tool revealed why the four winds of heaven were the key to identifying who battles who in the last days. I overcame a traditional roadblock—a belief commonly held on prophecy that had no scriptural support.

A GLIMPSE INTO THE NEAR FUTURE

Remember, chapters and numbering were added for us to locate scripture. There are no chapter divisions in the original text. In chapter nine, the angel Gabriel completes instructing Daniel on the revelation of seventy weeks. He ends in v27, and then we have chapter 10v1. Verse one summarizes all that is to come. It's a summary of chapters 10-12. Daniel is saying I get it. I now understand. In verse two and beyond, he reveals to the reader how that came to pass. The vision of chapter nine wasn't clear to Daniel. Gabriel had just announced that the glorious temple of Solomon would be rebuilt only to be destroyed again, that the Messiah would come only to be cut off.

Much darkness surrounded the future of his people. Chapter 10:14, the angel makes it clear. He said to Daniel," I have now come to make you understand what shall befall your people in the latter days."

Dan 11:2 And now will I show thee the truth. Behold, there shall stand up yet three kings in Persia, and the fourth shall be far richer than they all: and by his strength, through his riches, he shall stir up all against the realm of Grecia.

Most historians agree the four kings were: Cambyses from 530 to 521 BC, Darius the Great 521-486 BC, Xerxes 486–465 BC, and Artaxerxes 464–423 BC. Artaxerxes was by far the wealthiest, with over 120,000.000 Talents of bullion stored in the storehouses of Persepolis.

Verse three speaks about Alexander the Great, the Conqueror of the great Persian Empire, and most of the known world. Daniel received a vision concerning him in chapter eight, verse five, the notable goat from the west.

Dan 8:8 Therefore the goat waxed very great: and when he was strong, the great horn was broken; and from it came up four notable ones toward the four winds of heaven.

History tells us Alexander died in his prime at the age of thirty-two in Bagdad. The purpose of chapter eleven is to further explain and expound upon the vision of chapters eight and nine. Remember, in Chapter eight, God gives him a prelude to these four notable horns.

It also gives information on one of their decedents who will commit an abomination, defiling the temple. Antiochus Epiphanes was a Greek king of the Seleucid Empire who reigned over Syria from 175 BC until 164 BC. Some have mistaken this for the end-time scenario with the anti-Christ. This was a prelude to what was to come. The scripture in chapter eight clarifies that the reference of "the end" refers to their kingdom in that period.

Dan 8:17 So he came near where I stood: and when he came, I was afraid, and fell upon my face: but he said unto me,

Understand, O son of man: for at the time of **the end shall be the vision.**

The end of what? The vision he had just received, the violating of the temple, and the trampling of the host.

Dan 8:19 And he said, Behold, I will make thee know what shall be in **the last end of the indignation: for at the time appointed the end shall be...:23 And in the latter time of their kingdom,** when the transgressors have come to the full, a king of fierce countenance, and understanding dark sentences, shall stand up.

In chapter eleven, Daniel receives further information on the vision of the goat in chapter eight.

Dan 11:4 And when he shall stand up, his kingdom shall be broken, and shall be divided toward the **four winds of heaven;** and not to his posterity, nor according to his dominion which he ruled: for his kingdom shall be plucked up, **even for others beside those.**

The point is their kingdoms, "others beside those," would be plucked up, speaking of the king of fierce countenance. They weren't the last earthly empire; therefore, this is not the end of the age.

After Alexander's death, they divided his empire among his four generals (known in Latin as the Diadochi, the name they are still referenced, from the Greek, *Diadokhoi*, meaning "successors"): Lysimachus, Cassander, Ptolemy, and Seleucus.

This is a crucial point in understanding this chapter. The word of God has given us a double witness in the book of Daniel to ensure we recognize the identities of these successors. Two of these kingdoms in the last days will have epic confrontations—the kingdom of the north and the kingdom of the south. One will be the kingdom of the anti-Christ.

Dan 11:5 And the king of the south shall be strong, and one of his princes; and he shall be strong above him, and have dominion; his dominion shall be a great dominion. :6 And at the end of years they shall join themselves together; for the king's daughter of the south shall come to the king of the north to make an agreement: but she shall not retain the power of the arm; neither shall he stand, nor his arm: but she shall be given up, and they that brought her, and he that begat her, and he that strengthened her in these times.

Most commentaries identify the north and the south as the Seleucids and Ptolemy Dynasty because Israel is located between these two Dynasties north and south of Israel. This interpretation is not inspired by scripture. It ignores the facts the scriptures give us concerning these dynasties.

This has led to historical speculation that doesn't add up. For instance, the following verse speaks about the daughter of the king of the south's lineage. Here is a commonly accepted commentary on this verse.

Ptolemy Philadelphus, king of Egypt, shall marry his daughter Berenice to Antiochus Theos, king of Syria,'' who already had a wife called Laodice.

"Berenice shall come to the king of the north, to make an agreement, but it shall not hold: She shall not retain the power of the arm; neither she nor her posterity shall establish themselves in the kingdom of the north, neither shall Ptolemy her father, nor Antiochus, her husband (*between whom there was to be a great alliance*), stand, nor their arm, but she shall be given up and those that brought her," all that projected that unhappy marriage between her and Antiochus, which occasioned so much mischief, instead of producing a coalition between the northern and southern crowns, as was hoped. Antiochus divorced Berenice and took his former wife, Laodice, who soon after poisoned him and procured Berenice and her son to be murdered. (*Ref: Adam Clarks Commentary/Ellicott's Commentary*)

That's the problem. She has no roots. They murdered her only child. The scripture also makes it clear what nation the anti-Christ will come.

Dan 9:26 And after threescore and two weeks shall Messiah be cut off, but not for himself: and the **people of the prince that shall come shall destroy the city and the sanctuary**; and the end thereof shall be with a flood, and unto the end of the war desolations are determined.

The future emperor Titus of Rome destroyed the city and the sanctuary in 70AD. Neither the Seleucids nor Ptolemy Dynasties geographically line up with the Roman empire of the last days. I've heard it said the troops Rome used for this battle were mixed, a majority Egyptian and Arab, which disproves a Roman antichrist. The problem is that method of interpretation has no confirming pattern.

The Persian Empire consisted of a mixed multitude: the Medes, Persians, Bactrians, and Parthians, to name a few. Yet the angel tells Daniel:

Dan 8:20 The ram which thou sawest having two horns are the kings of Media and Persia.

That mixed military represented a nation and empire. That's who God recognized. Later it became the Persian Empire, the smaller of the two.

The key is the four winds of heaven. Dan 11:4 And when he shall stand up, his kingdom shall be broken, and shall be divided toward the four winds of heaven.

We have confirmation. **Dan 8:8**

The term "four winds" is used nine times in the Old and New Testaments. It represents Directions.

Ezek 37:9 Then said he unto me, Prophesy unto the wind, prophesy, son of man, and say to the wind, Thus saith the Lord GOD; **Come from the four winds**, O breath, and breathe upon these slain, that they may live.

This means that the winds came from four different directions, North, South, East, and West.

Mark 13:27 And then shall he send his angels, and shall gather together his **elect from the four winds**, from the uttermost part of the earth to the uttermost part of heaven.

God is giving what we know today as the four cardinal directions: North, South, East, and West. He was showing Daniel their location compared to one another and not Jerusalem. If the Seleucid Kingdom is the northern kingdom, there would be no eastern kingdom, just two western kingdoms. Daniel identifies one of the directions in Dan 11:5.

When you look at a map of when Alexander the Great's kingdom was divided, it's clear that they're divided into four Directions. The Ptolemy Dynasty is south. The Seleucids Dynasty lies to the east and eventually grows to be one of the most powerful of the four. The Cassander Dynasty lies to the west. The King of the North is **the Lysimachus Dynasty**. It comprised **Thrace**, a geographical and historical area in southeast Europe, now split between Bulgaria, Greece, and one quarter in western Turkey. It's bounded by the Balkan Mountains to the north, the Aegean Sea to the south, and the Black Sea to the east. It comprises southeastern Bulgaria (Northern Thrace), northeastern Greece (Western Thrace).

Most of the Lysimachus Dynasty today would be part of the European Union.

This lines up with scripture. The word identifies the anti-Christ empire in Dan 9:26 as previously covered as the empire of Rome or today the European Union.

We find another witness in Daniel Chapter two. Daniel Interprets three nations would "arise" after Babylon, each conquering the previous to become the dominant empire in its time. History makes it clear following Babylon was the Medes and Persians, then the Greeks, and following the Greeks were the Romans. Today this would be the European Union. The iron and clay feet of the Roman Empire, which I will comment more on later in this book.

The First Two significant players in Rumors, the last days' conflict found in Daniel chapter eleven, are **The European Union and The Egyptian Alliance**. Their allies will be covered later. We will also discover a significant unknown player added to the Egyptian alliance who will lead it.

THE MYSTERY BRANCH

Daniel brings us to an essential transition in **Dan 11:5...**

And the king of the south shall be strong, and one of his princes; and he shall be strong above him, and have dominion; his dominion shall be a great dominion.

In this verse, the focus is on the king of the South, Ptolemy I. We know this because the next verse refocuses on Him. Yet this extraordinary tribute to one of his princes comes off like a second thought or honorable mention to the point the author is slightly distracted from the main subject. I can't help but think of Jesus and the rich young ruler. Mark 10:21 Then Jesus beholding him loved him,

One of the greatest of the Ptolemy princes was Ptolemy 2 Philadelphus, his son.

He began his reign as co-regent with his father Ptolemy 1 between 288-285 BC. His accomplishments are mind-boggling. He completed a canal for his ships from the Nile to the Gulf of

Suez. He constructed the famous Pharos Lighthouse, also known as the lighthouse of Alexandria. It stood well over four hundred feet high and is considered one of the Seven Wonders of the World. He commissioned the translation of the Old Testament from Hebrew to Greek. This gave the world at that time access to the word of God. No longer was it exclusively for the Jews, but now all humanity could know hope and redemption. These are but a few of this leader's great works. (*Ref; aldokkan.com*)

No Ruler after him matches his accomplishments. I believe verse five helps us identify Ptolemy I and sets the tragic story in verse six.

Dan 11:6 And at the end of years they shall join themselves together; for **the king's daughter** of the south shall come to the king of the north to make an agreement: but she shall not retain the power of the arm; neither shall he stand, nor his arm: but she shall be given up, and they that brought her, and he that begat her, and he that strengthened her in these times.

The daughter of Ptolemy I that joined the Lysimachus Empire, King of the north, was Arsinoe II.
Arsinoe II Married Lysimachus in about 299 BC and became his third wife. They had three children together. Arsinoe conspired with half-brother Ptolemy Ceraunus against Lysimachus son by his first wife named Agathocles. They forged the lie of treason against Agathocles and Lysimachus had him executed. This caused political disfavor for Arsinoe II. The scripture tells us, but she shall not retain the power of the arm; neither shall he stand, nor his arm: but she shall be given up, and they that brought her, and he that begat her, and he that strengthened her in these times.

After the death of Lysimachus, she could not hold the kingdom herself but fled to Cassandreia and eventually married her co-conspirator Ptolemy Ceraunus. Her aged father, Ptolemy I, had died several years earlier, and her brother Ptolemy II was her current husband's replacement for the throne of Egypt. She would later have to flee with her eldest son Ptolemy Epigone from her new husband after conspiring against him. Creaunus executed her two younger children. She returned to Egypt and bore no more children.

The focus is now on the scripture's transitions. Many have recognized that Daniel in Chapter Eleven goes from Alexander the Greats Generals to the Last day's scenario with the anti-Christ. **There is a break in time from ancient civilization to the last days.** Let's clarify what a break in time is.

A lot of what is missed in Dan. 11 comes from the fact that God reveals the destiny of ancient Greece and then moves on to the battle of Armageddon in one chapter. How does that happen? Many have come up with clever Interpretations. Some say this is a spiritual Greece, or this is not a literal text.

The problem with that is Daniel gives historical background. He's speaking of actual battles and real people. Others pick a point and declare the transition begins in that verse.

REMEMBER THE RULES OF INTERPRETATION. There is always a witness or confirmation in scripture. What is often missed or overlooked is the BREAK IN TIME.

Example: Dan 11:7...*But out of a branch of her roots...*

If this sounds familiar, it's because you may recall a similarly common quoted verse.

The word "Branch" symbolizes lineage. In Isa 60:21, Thy people also shall be all righteous: they shall inherit the land forever, the branch of my planting, the work of my hands, that I may be glorified.

Job 18:16 His roots shall be dried up beneath, and above shall his branch be cut off.:17 His remembrance shall perish from the earth, and he shall have no name in the street.

Job gives us a natural and spiritual lesson about branches and roots. Job 14:7 For there is hope of a tree, if it be cut down, that it will sprout again, and that the tender branch thereof will not cease.:8 Though the root thereof wax old in the earth, and the stock thereof die in the ground;):9 Yet through the scent of water it will bud, and bring forth boughs like a plant.

Job reveals that though a tree dies and its stump dries out, the root can remain dormant for many years. Yet, at a hint of water, be renewed into a thriving branch. Just as the tree or vine symbolizes families and generations, the branch from the root comes later, representing future generations. A good illustration of this is:

Isa 11:1 And there shall come forth a rod out of the stem of Jesse, and a Branch shall grow out of his roots::2 And the spirit of the LORD shall rest upon him, the spirit of wisdom and understanding, the spirit of counsel and might, the spirit of knowledge and of the fear of the LORD

David is the rod from the stem of Jessie. From the root of David comes "The Branch," Jesus the Christ.

This verse goes from the time of David till the time of Jesus Christ. Not just any time. It goes all the way to the millennial kingdom. Jerm.23:5-6

The verse continues... Isa 11:6 "The wolf also shall dwell with the lamb, The leopard shall lie down with the young goat, The calf and the young lion and the fatling together; And a little child shall lead them.7 The cow and the bear shall graze; Their young ones shall lie down together; And the lion shall eat straw like the ox.:8 The nursing child shall play by the cobra's hole, And the weaned child shall put his hand in the viper's den.:9 They shall not hurt nor destroy in all My holy mountain, For the earth shall be full of the knowledge of the LORD As the waters cover the sea.

This phrase preludes a break in time, from King David's father and David, till Christ in the Millennial Kingdom. The biblical timeline is about events. The concluding of one and the beginning of another. We are not always given the time frame between them.

Dan 11:7 (says) But out of a branch of her roots... How much time does that represent? All the battles that take place after this deal with the last days and the anti-Christ. The flow is continuous without a break.

We can compare this to Rev17, which starts with the sixth ruler and ends with the Anti-Christ, who will rule twice. We see the same pattern here in Daniel 11.

The rest of Daniel focuses on "Her seed," the king of the south attacking the beast kingdom of the north.

The king of the north will come back years later with a larger army and defeat them. This will be the sixth leader of the beast kingdom because it names two more, and the second one mentioned is the antichrist. This is in line with Revelation Chapter 17. We will look at this in detail later. NOTE:

This scenario Daniel is revealing after verse six of chapter eleven never played out in history. The significant conflicts happened between the east and north; and south and east. The Seleucus Dynasty eventually absorbed most of the Northern Lysimachus Dynasty. Rome finally takes over the north and conquers them all. This is important because the identity of the kingdom of the south is what we know today as Egypt. Alexander's general Ptolemy, who took Alexander's body to Egypt, founded the Ptolemaic Empire. The ruling men of his line were all named Ptolemy, and the woman, Cleopatra. Remember what Daniel informs us.

Dan 11:4 And when he shall stand up, his kingdom shall be broken, and shall be divided toward the four winds of heaven; and not to his posterity, nor according to his dominion which he ruled: for his kingdom shall be plucked up, **even for others beside those.**

"Those" refers to his generals. They would not hold these kingdoms as history revealed. The Romans conquered them all. The purpose of illustrating the empires of Alexander's generals is to **provide a geological location identifying the nations involved in these end-time conflicts.**
Not all the nations of the last day's conflicts are mentioned in the book of Daniel. Daniel was told:

Dan 10:14 Now I am come to make thee understand what shall befall **thy people** in the latter days: for yet the vision is for many days.

This was a revelation about how Israel would be affected by these surrounding nations. John's account in the book of revelation gives a worldwide view of the period. Other players are mentioned.

Now let's look at this branch of her roots. The only surviving son of Arsinoe II was her eldest son Ptolemy Epigone. Arsinoe II fled to Egypt to Ptolemy II for protection against Ptolemy Ceraunus. Ptolemy Ceraunus' brief reign as king ended in 279 BC as he was captured and killed during the Gallic invasion of the Balkans led by <u>Bolgios</u>, who conducted a series of mass raids on the mainland Greece. Ptolemy (Epigone) by then was the oldest and only surviving son of Lysimachus. Ptolemy II gave Ptolemy (Epigone) a city in Asia Minor called Telmessos in Lycia to govern in his own right and establish his dynasty. Before being under Ptolemaic rule, the city of Telmessos was previously under the kingship of Ptolemy's late father, Lysimachus. Thus Ptolemy would become a client monarch and have a kingdom to rule under the Ptolemaic Kingdom. A surviving inscription from Telmessos dated from 258 BC reveals Ptolemy's arms accord with the Egyptian government. It shows that Ptolemy II made Ptolemy (Epigone) a Ptolemaic official in the area and was given a large estate by the Pharaoh. Ptolemy Epigone and his decedents ruled as a Ptolemaic Client King of Telmessos beginning in late 258 BC. Telmessos, the only root of Arsinoe II, today is known as **Fethiye Southwestern Turkey**.

THE SOUTHERN ALLIANCE/ ALL ROADS LEAD TO TURKEY

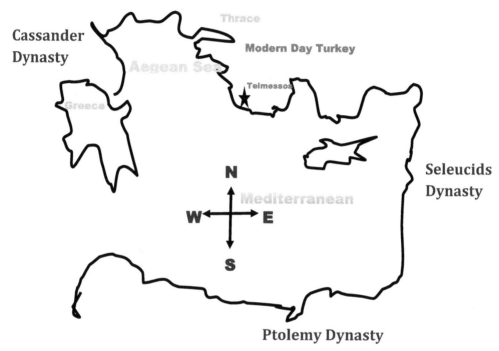

If the prophetic dots I've connected are correct, we see a Turkish-led coalition with Egypt in the end time's conflict. We know Egypt is not leading because Daniel tells us someone other than Egypt takes the lead.

Dan 11:7 "But from a branch of her roots one shall arise in his place, who shall come with an army, enter the fortress of the king of the north, and deal with them and prevail.:8 "**And he shall also carry their gods captive to Egypt,** with their princes and their precious articles of silver and gold; and he shall continue more years than the king of the north.

It doesn't name the allies of Egypt in Daniel. To find these, we must travel to Ezekiel. **Ezek 30:1-9** The prophecy in Ezekiel 30 is often overlooked because it's part of the Nebuchadnezzar prophecies. What's missed is the transition in verse 10, revealing the start of another prophecy. Verse1-9 concerns the last days, and v10 begins a prophecy concerning the Babylonian empire. To validate these nations are the south's allies in this period and to see these connections, it's essential to understand the prophetic event called **"The day of the lord."**

(Zec 14:7-9 KJV) But it shall be <u>one day</u> which shall be known to the LORD, not day, nor night: but it shall come to pass, that at evening time it shall be light. And it shall be in that day, that living waters shall go out from Jerusalem; half of them toward the former sea, and half of them toward the hinder sea: in summer and in winter shall it be. And the LORD shall be king over all the earth: in that day shall there be one LORD, and his name one.

This is the day that will bring an end to the battle of Armageddon. What's important to remember is it will be one day. God makes it clear so we don't misinterpret and says it's neither morning nor night, but it will happen in the evening. The focal point for this day is Jerusalem.

The city of Jerusalem will be under siege by foreign troops during the battle of Armageddon. There is no time frame for Armageddon. The word for "battle" is Polemos, which signifies warfare or campaign. It's the day Jesus returns with His saints. The mountains are moved out of place, and the Islands are no more. The major signs are an earthquake, the sun darkened, and the moon to blood.

Acts 2:20 The sun shall be turned into darkness, and the moon into blood, before that great and notable day of the Lord come.

There are many prophetic battles mentioned in scripture. The problem is what period do they represent. This is a vital part because it points to the last day's event, specifically Armageddon and the return of Christ.
The Day of The Lord ties together all the critical elements to understand the mystery of the last days.

2 Pet 3:10 But the day of the Lord will come as a thief in the night; in the which the heavens shall pass away with a great noise, and the elements shall melt with fervent heat, the earth also and the works that are therein shall be burned up.

Here are a few of the many scriptures in the Old Testament. Zec 14:1-14, Oba 1:15-17, *Isa 2:12, Isa 13:9-12, Joel 3:14-16, Amos 5:18-20,*

This time is also known in the scripture as a "Time of trouble. (Isa 33:2-3 KJV) O LORD, be gracious unto us; we have waited for thee: be thou their arm every morning, our salvation also in the time of trouble. At the noise of the tumult, the people fled; at the lifting up of thyself the nations were scattered.

With this foundation, we can now identify the Egyptian alliance. What's impressive is all roads lead to Turkey.

Ezek 30:3 For the day is near, even the day of the LORD is near, a cloudy day; it shall be the time of the heathen.:4 And the sword shall come upon Egypt, and great pain shall be in Ethiopia when the slain shall fall in Egypt, and they shall take away her multitude, and her foundations shall be broken down.:5 **Ethiopia, and Libya, and Lydia, and all the mingled people, and Chub, and the men of the land that is in league,** shall fall with them by the sword.

We See Ethiopia, Chub, Libya, Lydia, ancient western Turkey, the men of the league, and the mingled people. The word for mixed people means
(transverse threads of cloth); also a mixture, (or mongrel race): --Arabia, the Hebrew word is Ereb. We'll look at this ally in more detail later.

The nation of Chub is only mentioned once in the scriptures. The historical evidence on its location is vague. The Hebrew word Kub is defined as a country near Egypt - Chub. Possibly Algeria or Tunisia, yet it's close to the nation of Egypt, somewhere in North Africa.

Then there's, "The men of the land that is in the league" This Group speaks of a covenant or alliance with Egypt that is not given ancient geographical designation. They're not referred to as a nation but an individual group. These nations are military allies, so that would communicate this group of men has military influence.

This resembles groups today like Al-Qaeda and ISIS. (Islamic State of Iraq and Syria) So, in the end times, we see a militant group in alliance with Egypt.

Then we have Lydia. The Hebrew word "Luwd." Josephus, a Romano-Jewish historian, tells us Luwd was Lydia in his time or what we know today as western Turkey. **Reviewing 23 different translations of the Bible concerning this text, only 7 mentioned Lydia.** Over 70% ignored Turkey. The major commentaries also omit Lydia in this text. The reason may be because the newer translation followed the Prophetical trend of their time instead of unbiased interpretation. Therefore, I strongly recommend the King James Versions when doing research.

All these nations in Ezekiel 30 have one thing in common today: they're all Sunni Muslim-dominated nations. Egypt is the largest in the Arab world. Egypt has over 93 million people, 90% Muslim and over 90% Sunni. Ethiopia's Muslim population is 100% Sunni, but they are the second-largest religious group.

We see Ethiopia, Libya, and Turkey will be the main Allies with Egypt and a separatist militant group in alliance with Egypt. These will make up the alliances of "The King of the South," with the nation of Turkey taking the lead.

It's crucial to remember <u>Daniel was not pointing to the Ptolemy Dynasty as the end-time king of the south but the branch of their root</u> that points to Turkey.

CHAPTER 3)

THE MIGHTY GOG OF THE LAND OF MAGOG

Interpreting tool

Divine Revelation. Trust me when I tell you this journey has more to do with relationships than intellect.

God resists the proud but gives grace to the humble. Divine Revelation is when God causes us to see what's right in front of us. It's a gift. This was the Apostle Peter's- Jesus is more than a prophet moment.

Mat 16:17 And Jesus answered and said unto him, Blessed art thou, Simon Barjona: for <u>flesh and blood hath not revealed</u> it unto thee, but my Father which is in Heaven. The truth was always there. They simply didn't recognize it. We must check our motivation. Are we trying to discover the truth or trying to prove our point? One of the many gifts given to me is when God revealed the several places in the Old Testament the prophets speak of Gog, the ruler of Magog, and his evil intent toward Israel. It was always there. I just never recognized it.

THE MISPLACED PROPHECY

One of the greatest temptations in studying prophecy concerning the last days is to insert the prophecy of Gog and Magog into the tribulation timeline.

Almost all the books on last day's prophecy have Gog and the Magog nation as primary aggressors toward Israel during the tribulation, up to the final battle. Many have Gog playing the role of anti-Christ.

The problem is this piece of the puzzle never fits with the other scriptures concerning the same subject. One crucial issue: Where is Egypt? Daniel Chapter 11 makes it clear Egypt's a significant player in the king of the south alliances. It does not mention Egypt in Ezekiel 38 or 39 as an ally. In this prophecy, Egypt is not part of the attack on Israel, but her neighbors and allies of the south, Ethiopia and Libya, are with Persia, who is not listed in Ezekiel 30. That's because the scriptures reveal that Egypt has a unique role in the Millennium, which this prophecy concerns. We will discuss Egypt's role in the section on the Millennium.

Magog is **not** the king of the south. He is greater than the king of the south. Gomer, Togarmah (Turkey) follow him in the battle.

Ezek 38:7 Be thou prepared, and prepare for thyself, thou, and all thy company that are assembled unto thee, **and be thou a guard unto them.**

Magog is not Egypt because he comes from the north. He **is not** the anti-Christ King of the north because Daniel tells us at the end of Armageddon speaking of the antiChrist...,

Dan 11:45 And he shall plant the tabernacles of his palace between the seas in the glorious holy mountain, yet he shall come to his end, and none shall help him.

God's Holy Mountain is Jerusalem.

Dan 9:16 O Lord, according to all thy righteousness, I beseech thee, let thine anger and thy fury be turned away from thy city Jerusalem, thy holy mountain:

The Anti-Christ is firmly established between Jerusalem and the Mediterranean Sea. Gog of Magog is heading to the mountain of God, not making his last stand from it. Gog's motivation is the wealth of Israel. He's coming to take it. In Daniel chapter 11, the Anti-Christ already controls Israel's wealth and Temple before Armageddon ever starts.

Those who believe Ezekiel 38 is a preemptive strike before Armageddon must ask: If God protected Israel here, why not during Armageddon? (Dan 11:41/Rev 11:2) They must also ask, are all these nations destroyed before Armageddon?

WHO IS GOG?

So again, who is Gog of Magog? Where is the empire of Magog? This is one of the most controversial questions in Christianity today concerning prophecy.

Once we identify him, you will understand why he doesn't belong with the tribulation prophecies. I also hope clarity will come in determining the nation of Magog. Let's look at the prophecy.

Ezek 38:17 Thus saith the Lord GOD; Art thou he of whom I have spoken in old time by my servants **the prophets** of Israel,

which prophesied in those days many years that I would bring thee against them?

We know Gog is only mentioned once outside our text in the Old Testament. **1 Chr 5:4** The sons of Joel; Shemaiah his son, Gog his son, Shimei, his son.

This genealogy shows us he's the son of Joel, a descendent of Ruben. Nothing links him to the prophecy in Ezekiel chapter 38. Yet God reveals he has an appointment with judgment for the threats against His people and that it is well documented among His prophets. Where has Gog threatened the children of Israel? Where has God spoken of the luring for his destruction by His prophets?

The key is in the question. **"Art Thou he?"** Here God questions the very identity of Gog. He asked a question He knows the answer to for our benefit. Let's pull off the mask and expose the masquerade. **"Art Thou he ?"** The Lord was not addressing the man called Gog in this prophecy but the spirit behind the man.

God, through His prophets, gave proclamations of Judgments upon kings and kingdoms because of the harsh treatment of Israel. Yet, in several of these prophecies, God goes beyond speaking and addressing the ruler of a nation or kingdom. He, through His prophet, speaks to the spirit, motivating them. An excellent example of this is Tyrus, also known as the King of Tyre.

Ezek 26:2 Son of man, because that Tyrus hath said against Jerusalem, Aha, she is broken that was the gates of the people:

she is turned unto me: I shall be replenished, now she is laid waste:

Tyrus, in the spirit of evil, aimed to take advantage of a wounded Israel.

God's immediate response was Ezek 26:3 Therefore thus saith the Lord GOD; Behold, I am against thee, O Tyrus, and will cause many nations to come up against thee, as the sea causeth his waves to come up.

Later, Ezekiel prophesied this...Ezek 28:12 Son of man, take up a lamentation upon the king of Tyrus, and say unto him, Thus saith the Lord GOD;

Thou sealest up the sum, full of wisdom, and perfect in beauty.13 Thou hast been in Eden the garden of God; every precious stone was thy covering, the sardius, topaz, and the diamond, the beryl, the onyx, and the jasper, the sapphire, the emerald, and the carbuncle, and gold: the workmanship of thy tabrets and of thy pipes was prepared in thee in the day that thou wast created.14 <u>Thou art the anointed cherub</u> that covereth; and I have set thee so: thou wast upon the holy mountain of God; thou hast walked up and down in the midst of the stones of fire.15 Thou wast perfect in thy ways from the day that thou wast created, till iniquity was found in thee.16 By the multitude of thy merchandise they have filled the midst of thee with violence, and thou hast sinned: therefore I will cast thee as profane out of the mountain of God: and I will destroy thee, O covering cherub, from the midst of the stones of fire.17 Thine heart was lifted up because of thy beauty, thou hast corrupted thy wisdom by reason of thy brightness:

I will cast thee to the ground, I will lay thee before kings, that they may behold thee.

Satan cast from Heaven. Another prophecy concerns the King of Babylon.

Isa 14:4 That thou shalt take up this proverb against the king of Babylon, and say, How hath the oppressor ceased! the golden city ceased! 5 The LORD hath broken the staff of the wicked, and the sceptre of the rulers.6 He who smote the people in wrath with a continual stroke, he that ruled the nations in anger, is persecuted, and none hindereth.

Later, Isaiah speaking of the king of Babylon, prophesied this:

Isa 14:11 Thy pomp is brought down to the grave, and the noise of thy viols: the worm is spread under thee, and the worms cover thee.12 How art thou fallen from Heaven, O Lucifer, son of the morning! How art thou cut down to the ground, which didst weaken the nations!13 For thou hast said in thine heart, I will ascend into Heaven, I will exalt my throne above the stars of God: I will sit also upon the mount of the congregation, in the sides of the north.14 I will ascend above the heights of the clouds; I will be like the most High.15 Yet thou shalt be brought down to hell, to the sides of the pit.16 They that see thee shall narrowly look upon thee, and consider thee, saying, Is this the man that made the earth to tremble, that did shake kingdoms;17 That made the world as a wilderness, and destroyed the cities thereof; that opened not the house of his prisoners?18 All the kings of the nations, even all of them, lie in glory, every one in his own house.

20 <u>Thou shalt not be joined with them in burial</u>, because thou hast destroyed thy land, and slain thy people: the seed of evildoers shall never be renowned.

The devil's fall during the tribulation. Notice here, he's not cast down but cut down.

He is trying to ascend or retake Heaven. He has weakened the nations, destroyed their cities, and made the planet a wilderness. He has failed. Just as John spoke in the book of Revelation, he does not join them in burial.

Notice how this prophecy intertwines with the judgment of a man and simultaneously the devil himself.

This is the point. Satan always finds a surrogate to work through in his quest to destroy Israel. From the beginning in Gen 3:15, when God said:

And I will put enmity between thee and the woman, and between thy seed and her seed; it shall bruise thy head, and thou shalt bruise his heel.

The devil has tried to destroy that seed which we know today as Israel. We see throughout the writing of the prophets' time and again of attempts to destroy this nation. He has, throughout history, taken the hearts of some of the mightiest rulers to destroy the Hebrew people. Men lifted by pride, greed, and success, driven by an illogical hatred and passion for destroying a people without reason.

Who is Gog? **Gog is the devil's surrogate after the Millennium to destroy God's people**. It's his final act of defiance against the prophesied word of God.

Rev 20:7 And when the thousand years are expired, Satan shall be loosed out of his prison, 8 <u>And shall go out to deceive the nations which are in the four quarters of the earth, Gog and Magog, to gather them together to battle:</u> the number of whom is as the sand of the sea.9 And they went up on the breadth of the earth and compassed the camp of the saints about, and the beloved city: and fire came down from God out of Heaven, and devoured them 10 And the devil that deceived them was cast into the lake of fire and brimstone, where the beast and the false prophet are and shall be tormented day and night forever and ever.

This is in harmony with Ezekiel 38. Revelation 20 happens after the thousand-year reign in the New Jerusalem. Many read the account of Ezekiel chapter 38 but fail to read chapter 37. God gives Ezekiel a revelation in the valley of dry bones. This is the promise of restoring them to their land and more to their relationship with their Heavenly Father.

Ezek 37:14 And shall put my spirit in you, and ye shall live, and I shall place you in your own land: then shall ye know that I the LORD have spoken it, and performed it, saith the LORD.

Right after this, God speaks of the millennial Kingdom of the New Jerusalem.

Ezek 37:22 And I will make them one nation in the land upon the mountains of Israel; and <u>one king shall be king to them all:</u>

and they shall be no more two nations, neither shall they be divided into two kingdoms any more at all:23 Neither shall they defile themselves any more with their idols, nor with their detestable things, nor with any of their transgressions: but I will save them out of all their dwelling places, wherein they have sinned, and will cleanse them: so shall they be my people, and I will be their God.24 And David my servant shall be king over them; and they all shall have one shepherd: they shall also walk in my judgments, and observe my statutes, and do them.25 And they shall dwell in the land that I have given unto Jacob my servant, wherein your fathers have dwelt; and they shall dwell therein, even they, and their children, and their children's children for ever: and my servant David shall be their prince forever.26 Moreover I will make a covenant of peace with them; it shall be an everlasting covenant with them: and I will place them, and multiply them, and will set my sanctuary in the midst of them forevermore.27 My tabernacle also shall be with them: yea, I will be their God, and they shall be my people.

So, we have the valley of dry bones: the restoration of the Hebrew nation to its land. Then we have a picture of the Millennial Kingdom, followed by the Judgment of Gog of Magog. This is the exact order in the book of Revelation.

The Jewish people restored to God have a thousand years of perfect reign, and God supernaturally protects them from an attack of the world's armies led by Magog after Satan's loosed.

Let's take a closer look at Ezekiel 38.

Ezek 38:3 And say, Thus saith the Lord GOD; Behold, I am against thee, O Gog, the chief prince of Meshech and Tubal:...

Ezek 38:7 Be thou prepared, and prepare for thyself, thou, and all thy company that are assembled unto thee, and be thou a guard unto them.8 After many days thou shalt be visited: in the latter years thou shalt come into the land that is brought back from the sword, and is gathered out of many people, against the mountains of Israel, which have been always waste: but it is brought forth out of the nations, <u>and they shall dwell safely all of them</u>.9 Thou shalt ascend and come like a storm, thou shalt be like a cloud to cover the land, thou, and all thy bands, and many people with thee.10 Thus saith the Lord GOD; It shall also come to pass, that at the same time shall things come into thy mind, and thou shalt think an evil thought:11 And thou shalt say, <u>I will go up to the land of unwalled villages; I will go to them that are at rest</u>, **that dwell safely**, <u>all of them dwelling without walls, and having neither bars nor gates,</u>

During this period, the Hebrew people dwell safely. Since Israel became a nation, they have not lived safely. Even the book of Revelation 10 tells us the temple will be trampled by the gentiles for three and half years.

Ezekiel 38 says they would have no defense. Without walls, no bars, no gates, they are at rest. This is in step with Isaiah's vision of New Jerusalem.

Isa 65:19 I will rejoice in Jerusalem, And joy in My people; The voice of weeping shall no longer be heard in her, Nor the voice of crying.20 "No more shall an infant from there live but a few days, Nor an old man who has not fulfilled his days; For the child shall die one hundred years old, But the sinner being one hundred years old shall be accursed.21 They shall build houses and inhabit them;

They shall plant vineyards and eat their fruit.22 They shall not build and another inhabit; They shall not plant and another eat; For as the days of a tree, so shall be the days of My people, <u>And My elect shall long enjoy the work of their hands.</u>23 They shall not labor in vain, Nor bring forth children for trouble; For they shall be the descendants of the blessed of the LORD, And their offspring with them.24 "It shall come to pass That before they call, I will answer; And while they are still speaking, I will hear.25 The wolf and the lamb shall feed together, The lion shall eat straw like the ox, And dust shall be the serpent's food. <u>They shall not hurt nor destroy in all My holy mountain,"</u> Says the LORD.

We're even told in Zachariah that after the Day of the Lord, Israel will know peace.

Zec 14:11 And men shall dwell in it, and there shall be no more utter destruction, but Jerusalem **shall be safely inhabited.**

*It is clear that Ezekiel Chapter 38 doesn't happen in a time of tribulation.

*This tells us Gog becomes the devil's surrogate after he's released to destroy Israel.

*Finally, God is there. He has taken residence in the city.

Ezek 39:7 So will I make my holy name known in the midst of my people Israel; and I will not let them pollute my holy name any more: and the heathen shall know that **I am the LORD,** the Holy One **in Israel.** (The only use of this phrase in the scriptures usually is "**of Israel.**")

Rev 20:4 And I saw thrones, and they sat upon them, and judgment was given unto them: and I saw the souls of them that were beheaded for the witness of Jesus, and for the word of God, and which had not worshipped the beast, neither his image, neither had received his mark upon their foreheads, or in their hands; and they lived and reigned with Christ a thousand years.

NOTES ON THE CATASTROPHES

The evidence is overwhelmingly clear. Gog is a surrogate, and the placement is after a 1000yr reign. Yet, there are two issues I'd like to address that I believe are essential. One is the earthquake of Ezekiel 38.

Ezek 38:19 For in my jealousy and in the fire of my wrath have I spoken, Surely in that day there shall be a great shaking in the land of Israel; 20 So that the fishes of the sea, and the fowls of the Heaven, and the beasts of the field, and all creeping things that creep upon the earth, and all the men that are upon the face of the earth, shall shake at my presence, and the mountains shall be thrown down, and the steep places shall fall, and every wall shall fall to the ground.

This seems similar to the day of the Lord account. This is the day of the Lord account mentioned in Isaiah and Revelation.

Isa 34:2 For the indignation of the LORD is upon all nations, and his fury upon all their armies: he hath utterly destroyed them, he hath delivered them to the slaughter.:3 Their slain also shall be cast out, and their stink shall come up out of their carcases, and the mountains shall be melted with their blood. 4 And all the host of Heaven shall be dissolved,

48

and the heavens shall be rolled together as a scroll: and all their host shall fall down, as the leaf falleth off from the vine, and as a falling fig from the fig tree.

Rev 16:20 And every island fled away, and the <u>mountains were not found</u>.

The Greek word for <u>found </u>is "heurisko." It means to perceive, see, obtain. In Revelation, they couldn't locate the mountains. It's like they've been moved out of place. No doubt some might have disappeared altogether, but this event is not the same as Ezekiel. The mountains in Ezekiel are coming down. The point is mountains survive after the tribulation. The hills are beaten down and destroyed after the millennia.

The Second issue is The Lord's Feast to the fowls.

Ezek 39:4 Thou shalt fall upon the mountains of Israel, thou, and all thy bands, and the people that is with thee: I will give thee unto the ravenous birds of every sort, and to the beasts of the field to be devoured.:5 Thou shalt fall upon the open field: for I have spoken it, saith the Lord GOD.

Ezek 39:17 And, thou son of man, thus saith the Lord GOD; Speak unto every feathered fowl, and to every beast of the field, Assemble yourselves, and come; gather yourselves on every side to my sacrifice that I do sacrifice for you, even a great sacrifice upon the mountains of Israel, that ye may eat flesh, and drink blood.:18 Ye shall eat the flesh of the mighty, and drink the blood <u>of the princes of the earth</u>, of <u>rams, of lambs, and of goats, of bullocks, all of them fatlings of Bashan.</u>

Rev 19:18 That ye may eat the flesh of kings, and the flesh of captains, and the flesh of mighty men, and the flesh of horses, and of them that sit on them, and the flesh of all men, both free and bond, both small and great.

At first glance, these look similar, but they are not. I believe this is a continuation of the feast that began with the Mark of the Beast. The devil's surrogate of the tribulation and his followers. Notice the differences between the two. Revelation focuses on the man of war and judgment on the rebellious and disobedient. This is about wrath and deliverance, the rod of iron.

Rev 19:15 And out of his mouth goeth a sharp sword, that with it he should smite the nations: and he shall rule them with a rod of iron: and he treadeth the winepress of the fierceness and wrath of Almighty God.

Ezekiel's account seems about completion. Unlike Revelation, Ezekiel's focus is on livestock.

Bashan is the land of giants God caused Israel to defeat. Their land was plenteous. Their livestock was extremely healthy, perfect for sacrifice. It seems to imply that the livestock is symbolic of the mighty men and princes. Ezekiel shows a sacrifice, a type of brazen altar. It requires the Ram for a burnt offering. A burnt offering is for the satisfaction of God. It means" ascending as smoke." The others are all the animals required for a peace offering made by fire. Lev 3:1-17. The focus of the 1000-year reign is peace. The reign of the accuser has ended, the deceiver's influence destroyed, and God is pleased. On this battlefield, a great offering of peace is provided by the Heavenly Father.

Psa 37:20 But the wicked shall perish, and the enemies of the LORD shall be as the fat of lambs: they shall consume; into smoke shall they consume away.

WHERE IS THE LAND OF MAGOG

Now we know who Gog is, but where is the land of Magog. I believe the Bible interprets itself. We must go to the beginning.

Gen 10:2 The sons of Japheth; Gomer, and **Magog**, and Madai, and Javan, and **Tubal**, and **Meshech**, and Tiras :3 And the sons of Gomer; Ashkenaz, and Riphath, and Togarmah.

Magog, the grandson of Noah, became the chief prince of two of his Brothers. This is how Ezekiel refers to him.

Ezek 38:2 Son of man, set thy face against Gog, the land of Magog, the chief prince of Meshech and Tubal, and prophesy against him,

The word chief is the Hebrew word "Rosh or roshe." It's used 612 times in the Old Testament, and its interpretation in our text is head, as in leader. (Not Russia) The word prince is the Hebrew word for captain, Governor, or ruler. There was a bond between these three brothers, unlike the others. They stayed together. This also means their tribes became notable nations, Magog being the greatest. When you look at their geographical location by most historical records,

Tubal and Meshech in the time of Ezekiel would have been neighbors. Tubal would have been in the nation of Georgia and Meshech Northeastern Turkey.

Though these locations vary in some accounts, most place them in or near central and northeast Turkey. Magog's site is debatable. To have influence and lead, he would have to be near the others. Magog would be notable as he is the chief prince. The two popular theories place Magog in proximity to his brothers. One group places Magog in central Turkey, the other places Magog in Southern Russia, the Caucasus Mountains regions.

Two views I believe articulated this best I found online (*www.oxfordbiblechurch.co.uk*)

View 1)

Ethnologists, historians who track the migrations of people, tell us after the Flood, the Japhethites migrated from Asia Minor to the north, beyond the Caspian and Black Seas.

They settled in the area of Rosh that we know today as Russia. Wilhelm Gesenius, the world-class Hebrew scholar, said Gog is undoubtedly the Russians. He also identified Meshech as Moscow, the capital of modern Russia. Tubal, identified as Tobolsk, the earliest province in Asiatic Russia to be colonized and the city's name in which Peter the Great built the old fortress after the pattern of the Kremlin in Moscow. "Meshech was the founder of the Moschi, a barbarous people, who dwelt in the Moschian mountains."

He went on to say that the Greek name "Moschi," derived from the Hebrew 'Meshech', is the source of the name for the city of MOSCOW. In discussing Tubal, he said: "Tubal is the son of Japheth, founder of the Tibereni, a people dwelling on the Black Sea to the west of the Moschi." His conclusion was these people make up the modern Russian people.

View 2)

Another line of the study reveals that Meshech and Tubal are the ancient Moschi/Mushki and Tuvalu/Tibareni peoples who dwelled in the area around, primarily south of, the Black and Caspian Seas in Ezekiel's day. Meshech and Tubal are mentioned together in Ezekiel 27:13 as trading partners with ancient Tyre (modern Lebanon). Today these regions are in Turkey, possibly including parts of southern Russia and northern Iran. Meshech, located near what was known as Phrygia in central and western Asia Minor, while Tubal was located in eastern Asia Minor. So Meshech and Tubal from portions of modern Turkey. Herodotus, the 5th century BC Greek philosopher, mentioned Meshech and Tubal.

He identified them with the Sarmatians and Muscovites who lived in the ancient province of Pontus in northern Asia Minor, SE of the Black Sea [Histories IV], again pointing to modern Turkey. (End of article)

After countless hours of reading articles and historical accounts similar to this, one thing is clear. There's evidence of Magog in both Russia and Turkey. Artifacts show the ancient Magogites, called by the Greeks Scythians, existed in various parts of Russia.

The quote from the Historian Josephus I-6 concerning the Greek identity of the Scythians was broad. They considered everything north of the black sea, and Caucasus Mountain's from Rome to China as Scythian. It is important to interpret this text correctly. We must discover where these tribes settle during the times of Ezekiel's prophecy. Throughout the generations, there has been constant migration. God gave his prophets the geographical location of future nations using the nations they would recognize in their time. One plus is we have some well-established locations for the other ancient nations.

For all the arguments for a Turkish Magog, the allies of Magog are often overlooked.

Ezek 38:5 Persia, Ethiopia, and Libya with them; all of them with shield and helmet: 6 **Gomer (Central Turkey),** and all his bands; the house of **Togarmah (East Turkey) of the north quarters**, and all his bands: and many people with thee.

Ezekiel chapter 38 shows a divided turkey. In Ezekiel chapter 30, the prophecy mentions one nation, Lydia **(Western Turkey)**, which is not listed here.

My point is Turkey is already covered by these ancient landmarks and divided in this prophecy. Ezekiel sees ancient nations for landmarks, geographically for nations to come in his book. In Ezekiel 30, The day of the Lord, he sees a single Turkey. In Chapters 38 and 39, he sees a divided Turkey. Magog is unique from all listed in that God says," set thy face against Gog, **the land** of Magog,"

The Hebrew word for land here means common, country, earth, field, ground, land, nations, way, + wilderness, world. This language is not used toward others. It's also in the north quarter as Togarmah. The Hebrew word for north is "tsaphown," which means hidden, dark; used only of the north as a quarter (gloomy and unknown). This describes the Black and Caspian seas and mountain ranges of that area.

The nation of Magog is so massive it could be a guard to them all in battle. The process of elimination for a large nation north of Turkey (because central turkey is due north on a map) doesn't leave many options.

I believe this is the mighty Scythian people whose <u>burial mounds were found on the Caucasus mountains and were made during the time of Ezekiel</u>. The fierce bowman, mentioned by the Greek historian Herodotus, lived north beyond the Caspian and Black Seas who would dare challenge Cyrus the Great. A group of marauders became notable people and populated the territories from northeastern Europe to China. I believe Magog is the Father of the Russian people.

CHAPTER 4)

THE IDENTITY OF THE NORTHERN KINGDOM AND HIS ALLIES.

Interpreting tool

The key to all prophecy (The testimony of Jesus is the spirit of all prophecy) Rev 19:10. We have the words of Jesus in the Gospels and the narration of Jesus in the book of Revelation. The volume of all scripture speaks of him. (Heb10:7) Many prophecies could be placed in context and understood simply by hearing what Jesus had to say concerning them or applying the truth concerning Him.

A good example is an abomination that makes desolate. There are two mentioned in Daniel's book. The life of Jesus clarifies which of the two to look for.

ABOMINATION THAT MAKES DESOLATE

At this point, I believe we have identified the king of the north as the European Union or revised Roman Empire of today led by the anti-Christ. It's important to understand his role. He is the devil's surrogate for the tribulation period. Just as Gog will be the vessel of destruction after the millennial time frame, the vile one will execute the will of Satan before the millennial.

We must use various sources throughout the scriptures to understand his part in these events. As we look at the king of the north, remember we're speaking of an empire and an individual. This individual is easy to spot in scripture. One sign that sets him apart is he commits the **Abomination of Desolation**.

Dan 11:31 And arms shall stand on his part, and they shall pollute the sanctuary of strength, and shall take away the daily sacrifice, and they shall place the abomination that maketh desolate.

Dan 9:27 And he shall confirm the covenant with many for one week: and in the midst of the week he shall cause the sacrifice and the oblation to cease, and for the overspreading of abominations he shall make it desolate, even until the consummation, and that determined shall be poured upon the desolate.

Mat 24:15 When ye therefore shall see the abomination of desolation, spoken of by Daniel the prophet, stand in the holy place, (whoso readeth, let him understand:) 16 Then let them which be in Judaea flee into the mountains: 17 Let him which is on the housetop not come down to take anything out of his house: 18 Neither let him which is in the field return back to take his clothes. 19 And woe unto them that are with child, and to them that give suck in those days! 20 But pray ye that your flight be not in the winter, neither on the sabbath day 21 **For then shall be great tribulation**, such as was not since the beginning of the world to this time, no, **nor ever shall be**.

The word abomination means a covenant violation worthy of death. It often involves idolatry, and this one causes desolation. There is a particular judgment by God for violating His temple.

Ezek 5:11 Wherefore, as I live, saith the Lord GOD; Surely, **because thou hast defiled my sanctuary with all thy detestable things, and with all thine abominations,** therefore will I also diminish thee; neither shall mine eye spare, neither will I have any pity.12 **A third part of thee shall die with the pestilence,** and with **famine** shall they be consumed in the midst of thee: and <u>a third part shall fall by</u> **the sword** round about thee; <u>and I will scatter a third part into all the winds</u>, and I will draw out a sword after them.

The word for pestilence means a sense of destroying, plague. We find the description in the Seal Judgments in Revelation chapter six- War, Famine, and Death. Jesus tells us this will start the Great Tribulation.

The King of the North begins the great tribulation by violating the covenant of the sanctuary. We also find another sign.

HEAVENS VIEW

Daniel sees the coming anti-Christ in Daniel chapter 7called the little horn. God reveals to Daniel that there is an epic response from Heaven to this violation of the temple.

Dan 7:8 I considered the horns, and, behold, there came up among them another little horn, before whom **there were three of the first horns plucked up** by the roots: and, behold, in this horn were eyes like the eyes of man, and a mouth speaking great things. 9 <u>I beheld till the thrones were cast down, and the</u> <u>Ancient of days did sit, whose garment was white as snow, and</u> <u>the hair of his head like the pure wool:</u> his throne was like the fiery flame, and his wheels as burning fire.10 A fiery stream issued and came forth from before him:

thousand thousands ministered unto him, and ten thousand times ten thousand stood before him: the judgment was set, and the books were opened.

After the horn is revealed, then we see thrones cast down (SET IN PLACE). The picture of Christ in white garments and wool hair (Rev.1v14) is Christ, the judge. Note in Rev1v14 the two-edged sword precedes from his mouth.

(Psa 149:6-9 KJV) Let the high praises of God be in their mouth, and a two-edged sword in their hand; {7} To execute vengeance upon the heathen, and punishments upon the people; {8} To bind their kings with chains, and their nobles with fetters of iron; {9} To execute upon them the judgment written: this honour have all his saints. Praise ye the LORD (also Heb4v12, 2Thes2v7-8)

This event is known as **The Day of Christ**. Some might ask, what is the Day of Christ? The Day of Christ is closely related to the rapture.

(2 Th 2:1-4 KJV) Now we beseech you, brethren, by **the coming** of our Lord Jesus Christ, and by **our gathering** together unto him, {2} That ye be not soon shaken in mind, or be troubled, neither by spirit, nor by word, nor by letter as from us, as that the **day of Christ is at hand.** {3} Let no man deceive you by any means: for that day shall not come, except there come a falling away first, and that man of sin be revealed, the son of perdition; {4} **Who opposeth and exalteth himself above all that is called God, or that is worshipped; so that he as God sitteth in the temple of God,** showing himself that he is God.

Paul deals with two issues here: the "Coming" and the "Gathering." Paul tells us the Day of Christ happens after the man of sin is revealed. This is neither the resurrection of the church nor the Second Coming.

The Second Coming of Jesus shows the man of sin defeated. He states here the reveling is the abomination that makes desolate. (Math 24:15 Dan 9:27)

The Day of Christ begins with the revealing of the beast and the opening of the books. The opening of the books or scrolls begins the pronouncements of worldwide judgment. The Seal, Trumpet, and Vail judgments are mentioned in the book of Revelation. This was the concern of the Thessalonians. They thought they had missed the rapture and that the Judgments were about to begin. Paul tells us the Lord will consume the wicked two ways. The first was by the Spirit of His Mouth, later with the brightness of His coming.

(2 Th 2:7-8 KJV) For the mystery of iniquity doth already work: only he who now letteth will let, until he be taken out of the way. {8} And then shall that <u>Wicked be revealed, whom the Lord shall consume with the spirit of his mouth</u>, **and** shall destroy with the brightness of his coming:

(Dan 7:10 KJV) A fiery stream issued and came forth from before him: thousand thousands ministered unto him, and ten thousand times ten thousand stood before him: the judgment was set, and the books were opened. Compare with (Rev 4:5 KJV) & (Rev 5:6-8 KJV)

This is the Day of Christ. The beginning of the Great Tribulation.

THE PATTERN OF LAST REIGNS /TERM OF OFFICE

How the Beast Comes to Power:

There are two places that the Bible tells us directly, without symbolism, the beast's identity and how he will come to power: Daniel Chapter 11 and Revelation Chapter 17. The book of Revelation gives us a straightforward account of his succession. The book of Daniel 11:7-45 matches the account in the book of Revelation, adding battles and conspiracies. Many have tried to dissect Daniel's account, but it's next to impossible because, from v7-45, one story is told with no breaks in the text. It begins by revealing the king of the south and his exploits. Daniel 11v15 shifts the focus from the king of the south to the king of the north. It covers the current leader and his two successors. This is important because Daniel's account doesn't reveal how many kings will rule the north. God brings us in at a particular time that covers these last three Kings.

In Daniel chapter twelve, we see the resurrection of the just and unjust at the end of the tribulation. This is the parables Jesus gave us of the wheat and tares and the sheep and goats. At this point, it's over. Daniel's account of the vile one ends. John in the book of Revelation also focuses on the final three leaders of the end-time Beast kingdom.

Dan 11:15 So the king of the north shall come, and cast up a mount, and take the most fenced cities: and the arms of the south shall not withstand, neither his chosen people, neither shall there be any strength to withstand... 19 Then he shall turn his face toward the fort of his own land: but **he shall stumble and fall, and not be found...** 20 Then shall stand up **in his estate a raiser of taxes in the glory of the kingdom: but within few days he shall be destroyed,** neither in anger, nor in battle.... 21 And **in his estate shall stand up a vile person,** to whom they shall not give the honour of the kingdom: but he shall come in peaceably, and obtain the kingdom by flatteries.

Compare to Revelation 17

61

Rev 17:9 And here is the mind which hath wisdom. The seven heads are seven mountains, on which the woman sitteth.10 **And there are seven kings: five are fallen, and one is, and the other is not yet come**; and when he cometh, he must continue **a short space**... 11 And **the beast** that was, and is not, even **he is the eighth, and is of the seven**, and goeth into perdition.

There is a vitally important reason God begins at this point in history. Why does he cover the reigns of the last three leaders of the beast kingdom? What is so important about this time that God covers it in the two most prophetic books of the scriptures and gives us both an Old and New Testament witness?

One it identifies for the tribulation generation, the Anti-christ. He has two reigns, according to John's account. He will be the only one to do so as the Eighth and the last ruler. He commits the breaking of the holy covenant in Daniel 11 that initiates the Great Tribulation. **Secondly,** I believe what we're witnessing here is the restart of the time clock for the final week of Daniel's prophecy of seventy weeks.

If you're a student of prophecy, you know there is a break in time between week sixty-nine and seventy. This break is called the Time of the Gentiles.

Isa 11:10 And in that day there shall be a root of Jesse, which shall stand for an ensign of the people; to it shall the Gentiles seek: and his rest shall be glorious. Also...Isa 42:6

God's promise of redemption was not only for the Jew but for all humanity. We know that day came on the day of Pentecost, the birthing of the church and a New Covenant with God the Father. This does not mean the covenant promises God made concerning Jewish Destiny in the Old Covenant are forgotten.

Rom 11:25 For I would not, brethren, that ye should be ignorant of this mystery, lest ye should be wise in your own conceits; that blindness in part is happened to Israel, until the fulness of the Gentiles be come in. :26 And so all Israel shall be saved: as it is written, There shall come out of Sion the Deliverer, and shall turn away ungodliness from Jacob

These events beginning in Dan 11:7 are part of the last seven years before Jesus takes possession of the planet and takes His place as king.

Let's do the math: Dan 9:27 tells us the timeline for the covenant is seven years. (The final week) We have no idea how long the events leading up to and completing the first two conflict takes in Dan 11. After the first conflict, troops were removed from the north to Egypt, then back home. After a cooling period, troops were redeployed into another war.

The first major clue is the Sixth King of the north's comeback takes several years after the south's attack in v13. In v19, he begins a campaign against the Iles and is taken out shortly after this. King seven has a brief life, a few days to a few weeks. We have no actual periods, but these events estimate around 2 ½ to 3 years. Then Eight King (the anti-Christ) Reign begins with a significant conflict. We have no time frame for this. After his second conflict, he will commit the abomination in v31. Daniel tells us this happens 3 ½ years after they make the original covenant. That means the rest of this narration after the abomination that makes desolate in chapter 11 occurs in a 3 ½ year time frame, ending with the anti-Christ fall. Working backward, we know the covenant being broken to its creation is 3 ½ years. The word covenant is used six times in the book of Daniel. Once in his prayer to God, the other five times surrounding the anti-Christ. Dan 11:22 Hints to us the covenant was already in effect and made before the Last King of the North came on the scene.

The king of the south's intro until the anti-Christ violation covers most if not all the first 3 ½ years of this covenant. More years may be covered between v7 and the abomination in v31. One thing I can say for sure. **God begins this narration with the 6th king to show us these elements of the final week of Daniel 9v27.**

The math proves a minimum of six years realistically, that's not including calculating the length of all the battles we just covered.

Dan 9:24 Seventy weeks are determined upon thy people and upon thy holy city, to finish the transgression, and to make an end of sins, and to make reconciliation for iniquity, and to bring in everlasting righteousness, and to seal up the vision and prophecy, and to anoint the most Holy. These are called sabbatical years. (Lev.25:8)

THE SPIRIT OF THE BEAST

Prov 29:2 When the righteous are in authority, the people rejoice: but when the wicked beareth rule, the people mourn.

The final Identifier of the beast is his wicked month of blasphemies and the persecution of end-time saints. This is the spirit of anti-Christ. This is a constant struggle we find in scripture and see growing today.

Rev 13:6 And he **opened his mouth in blasphemy** against God, to blaspheme his name, and his tabernacle, and them that dwell in Heaven. 7 And it was given unto him to **make war with the saints,** and to overcome them: and power was given him **over all kindreds, and tongues, and nations.**

Dan 11:35 And some of them of understanding **shall fall**, to try them, and to purge, and to make them white, even to the time of the end: because it is yet for a time appointed. 36 And the king shall do according to his will; and he shall exalt himself, and magnify himself above every god, **and shall speak marvellous things against the God of gods,** and shall prosper till the indignation be accomplished: for that that is determined shall be done.

Dan 7:8 I considered the horns, and, behold, there came up among them another little horn, before whom **there were three of the first horns plucked up** by the roots: and, behold, in this horn were eyes like the eyes of man, and a mouth speaking great things. Dan 7:25 And he shall speak great words against the most High, and shall wear out the saints of the Most High.

The patterns in the above text are clear. The spirit of anti-Christ is an intense hatred for all that is Christ-like or Hebrew. What's also important to recognize is the progression. To secure his domination, he must remove believers. All the wars on the planet seemed to cease in Daniel chapter eleven for one purpose, which begins in verse 31, the persecution and murder of the saints. George Friedman, in his book "Flashpoints" ...

"World War I redefined what was reasonable in terms of revolutions. It eliminated boundaries to the inherently boundless processes, and it eradicated limitations on imaginable casualties. **It also undermined the institutions that might have held the slaughter in check, such as churches and families**, as well as sheer common sense." (End of excerpt)

They rated WWI as one of the deadliest conflicts in human history. Eighteen million were killed and 21 million wounded. These numbers will not compare with what's coming.

The influence of Christianity in society is a ballast of common sense that promotes family and stability. The spirit of anti-Christ promotes conflict and perversion.

They must remove one so the other can flourish.

FEET OF IRON AND CLAY

The Northern Empire is unlike any empire mentioned in scripture. In the book of Revelation Chapter 13, we see the transition from legs of iron to the feet of iron and clay.

Rev 13:1 And I stood upon the sand of the sea, and saw a beast rise up out of the sea, having seven heads and ten horns, and upon his horns ten crowns, and upon his heads the name of blasphemy.2 And the beast which I saw was like unto a leopard, and his feet were as the feet of a bear, and his mouth as the mouth of a lion: and the dragon gave him his power, and his seat, and great authority.

In Daniel chapter seven, he receives a vision of four great kingdoms that would arise from the earth.

Dan 7:4-7 The first was like a lion,... second, like to a bear,.. leopard... and behold a fourth beast, dreadful and terrible, and strong exceedingly; and it had great iron teeth: it devoured and broke in pieces, and stamped the residue with the feet of it: and it was diverse from all the beasts that were before it....

The angel tells Daniel the fourth beast will exist into the tribulation period, but the first three empires fade into history.

Dan 7:12 As concerning the rest of the beasts, they had their dominion taken away: yet their lives were prolonged for a season and time.

The word dominion in Hebrew means empire or rule. The scriptures reveal their rules would end, but their peoples and culture would be spared. Their identity would be intact for a season. In John's vision, the beast of Revelation chapter 13 has remnants of the former ruling empires. We will investigate this further, but first, let's identify the kingdoms.

In Daniel chapter two, God gives Nebuchadnezzar a dream about four kingdoms. The dream revealed a man's image. The head was of gold, the chest and arms of silver, the stomach and thighs of bronze, and the legs of iron with the toes being iron and clay.

Dan 2:39 And after thee shall arise another kingdom inferior to thee, and another third kingdom of brass, which shall **bear rule over all the earth.** 40 And the fourth kingdom shall be strong as iron: forasmuch as iron breaketh in pieces and subdueth all things: and as iron that breaketh all these, shall it break in pieces and bruise. 41 And whereas thou sawest the feet and toes, part of potters' clay, and part of iron, the kingdom shall be divided; but there shall be in it of the strength of the iron, forasmuch as thou sawest the iron mixed with miry clay. Dan 2:44 And in the days of these kings shall the God of Heaven set up a kingdom, which shall never be destroyed: and the kingdom shall not be left to other people, but it shall break in pieces and consume all these kingdoms, and it shall stand forever.

Again, we see the fourth kingdom extends to the return of Christ. Daniel answers this mystery in chapter five with the invasion of the Media and Persia. Babylon was the head of gold, and the Meads and Persians were the chest and arms of silver. Then God revealed to Daniel who would succeed the Persians; Alexander the Great, the "he-goat "of the Grecian empire. The Greeks are the stomach and thighs of brass. This is confirmed again in chapter 11.

Dan 11:2 And now will I show thee the truth. Behold, there shall stand up yet three kings in Persia; and the fourth shall be far richer than they all: and by his strength through his riches he shall stir up all against the realm of Grecia. 3 And a mighty king shall stand up, that shall rule with great dominion, and do according to his will.

As we see, the visions of Nebuchadnezzar's image and the vision of the beast show the consecutive conquest of empires. One after the other and stops with the last. The next great empire that overcomes the Greeks is the Roman Empire. This is the Iron legs empire and today's Iron mixed with clay. Rome was the fourth kingdom of iron and the fourth beast that conquered the Greeks. So, who defeated the Romans?

The Roman Empire, as history records, was never conquered. Even during the time of the great Ottoman Empire. It declined and suffered attacks by the barbarians over time and civil wars and eventually lost its political power over its territories. After the great Constantine, it became a religious empire through the Vatican with power that reached greater than any religion in history. It has influence and favor with governments around the globe. What we see today, believers of past generations could only hope to see.

The Roman Empire of Iron legs has passed. We live in the day of a new empire of iron and clay.

One of the monumental mistakes that can be made is interpreting the beast of Daniel as the beast of John. The beast of Daniel was a young, vibrant Rome of Iron Legs. The Beast of John is the End-time revised Rome of Iron and clay feet. Look at the difference between the beast of John and the beast of Daniel. Johns has seven heads, and Daniel has one. Daniel has ten horns which equal kings that belong to the kingdom. John's beast has ten horns that are not part of his kingdom. Rev.17 & Dan. 7:24

Dan 2:41 And whereas thou sawest the feet and toes, part of potters' clay, and part of iron, the kingdom shall be divided; but there shall be in it of the strength of the iron, forasmuch as thou sawest the iron mixed with miry clay. 42 And as the toes of the feet were part of iron, and part of clay, so the kingdom shall be partly strong, and partly broken. 43 And whereas thou sawest iron mixed with miry clay, they shall **mingle themselves with the seed of men:** but they shall not cleave one to another, even as iron is not mixed with clay.

If you remember the pattern, we discovered earlier that mingled people represented foreign groups within a nation. This is used several times in scripture. Exo 12:38 speaks about the mixed multitude that went out of Egypt with the children of Israel. This identifies them as a foreign group within the Israeli population. In Jer 50:37, it's the mingled people of Babylon. The same situation. They represent foreign groups in the Babylonian empire. The unifying culture of Roman iron is mixed with foreign cultures, clay. What better picture of today's European Union. This is the King of the North.

What is Culture?

Merriam-Webster dictionary/culture: the beliefs, customs, arts, etc., of a particular society, group, place, or time. : **a particular society that has its own beliefs, ways of life,**

art, etc.: a way of thinking, behaving, or working that exists in a place or organization

In John's vision, the beast of Revelation chapter 13 has remnants of the former ruling empires. The likeness of a Lion (Babylonian Empire), bear (Media and Persian Empire), and leopard (The Greek Empire). Revelation 13 says it looks Greek, which is the foundation of Roman government and architecture. The feet were like the Persian Empire.

The Persians were known foremost for their communication and transportation. Their engineering ability was like no other. Finally, it has a mouth like a lion, Babylon the golden head of all empires and mother of all false religions.

This beast has incorporated aspects of the previous empires, peoples, and cultures.

THE HARLOT

(Rev 17:5-7 KJV) And upon her forehead was a name written, MYSTERY, BABYLON THE GREAT, THE MOTHER OF HARLOTS AND ABOMINATIONS OF THE EARTH. And I saw the woman drunken with the blood of the saints, and with the blood of the martyrs of Jesus: and when I saw her, I wondered with great admiration. And the angel said unto me, Wherefore didst thou marvel? I will tell thee the mystery of the woman, and of the beast that carrieth her, which hath the seven heads and ten horns.

Interpreting tool

In proving a symbol, look for **figurative** examples. The word of God is consistent in its symbolism. The Holy Spirit took nothing to chance. Example = silver often refers to precious metal.

It is used to make many things in scripture, from utensils to poles. To identify any symbolic meaning, you must find a figurative pattern of usage, which is a logical interpretation of all the symbolic language uses of that word. It should be the same in both Testaments. Here's a few: (Gen 37:28, Lev 27, Judg 16:5, Mat 26:15) Joseph, Samson, Children of Israel, and Jesus had a silver value placed on their lives. Symbolically silver represents a value placed on man. As we look deeper, we see it's the cost of redemption. The word redemption in Greek and Hebrew are similar, meaning something exchanged for payment, for ransom, or riddance. There are times the scripture will give you the definition of a **symbol**. For example, the "blood" is symbolic of life. (Lev 17:11-14) and Leaven or Yeast symbolizes doctrine or belief system. (Math 16:6)

Rev17v.5 & Rev 17v18 tell us that the Harlot is a "**city**" that reigns over the Kings of Earth. She is carried by the beast of the revised Roman Empire, and she (the city) sits on seven mountains. (Rev.17v9) Commentators debate whether this is Babylon or Rome. I've heard some say this is a spiritual manifestation of the Babylonian religious system. This is an excellent time to recall the rules of interpretation, figurative and literal interpretations. If Revelation 17 symbolism seems uncertain, we must also recognize that chapter 18 completes the picture. It tells us Mystery Babylon is a port city set on fire. This is a city. The word of God is consistent. In both chapters, it's a city and clarifies this in chapter 18. Another hint is she's drunk with the blood of the martyrs of Jesus Christ.

Mystery Babylon, the Mother of Harlots, began in Gen ch11 at the tower of Babel.

The first recorded false religion sought to unite all humanity under one banner: self-glory. (Gen 11v4) This is the basis of all false religion, to divert trust in the true and the living God and trust in man's ability. Though God scattered the people, the tenets of this religion have survived history, and we see a reemergence of her global influence in the latter days. The roots of this religion are based on mother and son worship. This folklore begins with Nimrod and his mother, Semiramis. Semiramis became the Babylonian "Queen of Heaven," and Nimrod, under various names, became the "divine son of Heaven the false Messiah, son of Baal the Sun-god. Their names throughout history have changed. Isis and Horus, Ashtoreth and Tamuz (Ezekiel 8:14), Devaki and Chrisna, plus many more. The foundational tenets are the same. **A study of the religion of ancient Babylon revealed this**:

Temples and chapels were dedicated to one deity or another. Babylon, for example, possessed more than 50 temples in Chaldean times (8th to 6th century BC). Temple's services were generally conducted in open courts containing fountains for ablution and altars for sacrifices. The cella, or inner part of the temple, in which the deity's statue stood on a pedestal in a particular niche, was the holy of holies. Only the high priest and other privileged members of the clergy and court were permitted to enter it. In the temple complexes of the larger cities, a ziggurat, or staged tower, was often built, crowned by a small sanctuary, which was reserved for the all-important sacred – marriage ceremony celebrated in connection with the new – year festival.

The upkeep of the major Babylonian temples required significant revenues, provided primarily by gifts and endowments from the court and the wealthy. Some of the major Babylonian temples accumulated immense wealth and possessed large estates and factories employing large numbers of serfs and slaves in the centuries. Primarily, however, the temple was the house of God.

The deity's needs were provided per ancient rites, and impressive ceremonies carried out by a vast institutionalized clergy. The latter was comprised of high priests, sacrifice priests, musicians, singers, magicians, soothsayers, diviners, dream interpreters, astrologers, female devotees, and hierodules (temple slaves).

Sacrifices, offered daily, consisted of animal and vegetable foods, libations of water, wine, and beer, and the burning of incense. Numerous annual and monthly festivals were held, including a feast to celebrate the new moon. The most crucial celebration was the new year at the spring equinox; it was known as the Akitu festival because some of its more esoteric rituals was enacted in Akitu, Marduk's shrine outside of Babylon. The festival lasted 11 days and included such rites as purification, sacrifice, propitiation, penance, absolution, and colorful processions. The culmination was probably the sacred – marriage ceremony previously mentioned, which took place in the sanctuary crowning the ziggurat Beliefs.

Babylonian documents indicate that the ethical and moral beliefs of the people stressed goodness and truth, law and order, justice and freedom, wisdom and learning, and courage and loyalty. Mercy and compassion were espoused, and special protection was accorded to widows, orphans, refugees, the poor, and the oppressed. Immoral and unethical acts were considered transgressions against the gods and the divine order and were believed to be punishable by the gods accordingly.

No one was without sin, and therefore all suffering was held to be deserved. The proper course for Babylonians unhappy with their condition in life was not to argue and complain but to plead and wail, lament and confess their inevitable sins and failings before their personal God, who acted as their mediator in the assembly of the great gods.

(Encarta Encyclopedia 1998 version.)

HER IDENTITY

The world is dominated by religions that are remarkably similar to this Babylonian model of Idol (statue) worship. Erection of specialized temples for certain rites and ceremonies, special rites for purification, penance, and absolution by priests, wailing and lamenting for a personal favor from a deity are common traits of religions worldwide.

(Rev 17:1 KJV) And there came one of the seven angels which had the seven vials, and talked with me, saying unto me, Come hither; I will show unto thee the judgment of the great whore that sitteth upon many waters:

...:15 And he saith unto me, The waters which thou sawest, where the whore sitteth, are peoples, and multitudes, and nations, and tongues.

Only one church in Europe has crossed racial barriers, languages and has branches around the world. Only one influences governments around the world. No Protestant or Islamic institution has this influence to date.

(Rev 17:9 KJV) And here is the mind which hath wisdom. The seven heads are seven mountains, on which the woman sitteth.

Only one worldwide religion with this influence has its headquarters with a city on seven hills. Those hills are Capitoline, Quirinal, Viminal, Esquiline, Caelian, Aventurine, and Palatine, which make up Rome's city limit boundaries. Idols are not part of Christian worship; neither is praying to dead saints. Isa 8v19-20. Yet the Babylonians had a God for every occasion; travel, athletics, etc., over 5000.

The mystery religion has practices that identify with most religions and are easily adapted.

That's why she is the **Mother of Harlots**. What makes her unique is she is identified as being Christian. This is why fornication is implied, mixing the truth of God's word with **pagan practices**. The practice of such things is sin in the eyes of God. Only one religious' institution in Western Europe fits the description of Rev.17. Christians have one mediator. (1Tim2v5) No priest or Pope can regulate God's forgiveness for the dead nor mediate between God and man.

Christian worship doesn't revolve around temples. (Acts17v24 & 1Cor3v16) In Babylonian worship, the temple and religious buildings were believed to house the presence of God. The building became an Image *(Idol)*, a focus of worship. Indulgences *(Paying for the sins on the dead)* doing penance, wailing, and lamenting *(Self-induced suffering for favor)* is not only non-Christian but an insult to the blood of Jesus Christ! Hundreds of thousands of Protestant Christian were murdered during the reign of the Popes. *Ref (Ralph Woodrow Babylon Mystery Religion.)*

The word of God spends two chapters to ensure she is correctly identified. God's opinion of her is made clear, along with her judgment. This seems to be a major issue concerning the judgment of God, and we have this warning.

(Rev 18:4-5 KJV) And I heard another voice from Heaven, saying, <u>Come out of her, my people,</u> that ye be not partakers of her sins, and that ye receive not of her plagues. {5} For her sins have reached unto Heaven, and God hath remembered her iniquities

Believers in Jesus Christ would not mistake Buddhism or Islam for authentic institutions of their faith. However, Babylonian base religions often are. This religion will be the dominant religion of the beast's kingdom. Believers in this system will find it hard to separate themselves from the seductive tradition of this **mother and son worship** Babylonian religion. Failing to understand the freedom that the Blood of Jesus purchases, they insult it with self-flagellation and pennants as if we could purchase God's Love and Mercy.

Replacing a relationship with the Heavenly Father with obligatory rituals, not realizing praying to objects, symbols, and the holy mother is not faith but idolatry. In His great mercy, God sends messengers to call them out to offer them light for darkness.

THE FALSE PROPHET

(Rev 13:11-12 KJV) And I beheld another beast coming up out of the earth; and he had two horns like a lamb, and he spake as a dragon. {12} And he exerciseth all the power of the first beast before him, and causeth the earth and them which dwell therein to worship the first beast, whose deadly wound was healed.

Who is this mysterious beast? Who are these mysterious nations? Yes, nations. If the first beast represents a kingdom and leaders, which has been true of past metaphors, why would this one be different? The horns in scripture represent individual leaders or kings. Those kings also represent Nations. *(Dan 8:20)* This is a dominating ruling kingdom in the same period as the first beast. It comes from the earth. Meaning it's made up of other nations. The first beast comes from the Mediterranean sea, which relates to Daniel's original beast. (Dan. 7v3) This beast is not part of the original nations that formed around the Mediterranean.

76

This beast is **a combination of two kings and kingdoms** (two horns). They look like a lamb. This is symbolic of Jesus Christ. *John1v29. Acts.8v32, 1Pet.19v20.*

The reference of a lamb happens thirty-one times in the New Testament. If you minus out this text, every reference refers to the lamb of God Jesus Christ. John received Revelation, heard the reference twenty-seven times in the book of revelations. Yet we are told it speaks like a dragon, the devil. It looks Christian but speaks like a dragon. How does a dragon speak? The symbolism of the dragon in scripture is first referenced to **an ancient sea monster.** To understand a Biblical reference for this, you would have to go back to the first mention and the oldest book of the Bible- Job. The dragon is called leviathan... Job 41:1 Canst thou draw out leviathan with an hook?... Job 41:19 Out of his mouth go burning lamps, and sparks of fire leap out. How does a dragon speak? With words of fire.

Job 41:34 He beholdeth all high things..: <u>he is a king over all the children of pride</u>.

Ezek 29:3 Speak, and say, Thus saith the Lord GOD; Behold, I am against thee, Pharaoh king of Egypt, the great dragon that lieth in the midst of his rivers, which hath said, **My river is mine own, and I have made it for myself.**

The leading attribute is pride—the supreme feature of Satan. In the New Testament, the word dragon is used thirteen times. Twelve out of the thirteen times is a direct reference to Satan. The only other time is in our text. "Speaks like a dragon." This reveals that though he differs from the first beast, they are linked. He is the voice of the first beast. He speaks deceiving propaganda to promote the agenda of the first.

THE POWER OF THE PROPHET

CONTROLLING WHAT'S HEARD

False prophets in the scripture deceived the people with their words by creating a false narrative. Often God would rebuke them, saying this was not my direction. I have not spoken by them. They were the masters of propaganda at times leading whole armies to their defeat. The method of communication today is not a voice in the wilderness but the media. The false prophet will be a master of the press, controlling what is heard and what is spoken.

In a November 2017 discussion at the Stanford Graduate School of Business, Former Facebook Vice President Chamath Palihapitiya revealed he feels "tremendous guilt" over his role in heading a company aiding the destruction of society. What did he mean by this? Here are a few quotes from that discussion.

"The short-term, dopamine-driven feedback loops we've created are destroying how society works," Palihapitiya said, pointing to the insatiable need for "hearts, likes, thumbs-up."

"No civil discourse, no cooperation; misinformation, mistruth. And it's not an American problem — this is not about Russian ads. This is a global problem," He goes on to say, "So we are in a really bad state of affairs right now, in my opinion. It is eroding the core foundations of how people behave by and between each other."

Palihapitiya also highlighted how social media can manipulate mob mentality by referring to an incident in which seven Indian people were lynched due to a WhatsApp hoax.

"That's what we're dealing with," he said. "And imagine taking that to the extreme, where bad actors can now manipulate large swathes of people to do anything you want. It's just a really, really bad state of affairs."

"And we compound the problem, right? We curate our lives around this perceived sense of perfection, because we get rewarded in these short-term signals – hearts, likes, thumbs up – and we conflate that with value, and we conflate it with the truth. And instead what it is, **is fake, brittle popularity** that's short-term and that leaves you even more – and admit it – vacant and empty before you did it, because then it forces you into this vicious cycle where you're like, **'What's the next thing I need to do now? Because I need it back.'** Think about that compounded by two billion people, and then think about how people react then to the perceptions of others."

"Your behaviors, you don't realize it, but you are being programmed," Palihapitiya said. "It was unintentional, but now you got to decide how much you are willing to give up, how much of your intellectual independence.

Similar to how Apple's Steve Jobs didn't allow his children to use Ipads, Palihapitiya, referring to Facebook, said his children aren't allowed to use it. He went on to say, "The thought process that went into building these applications,

Facebook, being the first of them, was all about **"How do we consume as much of your time and conscious attention as possible?"'**

He goes on to say...."I don't know if I really understood the consequences of what I was saying, because [of] the unintended consequences of a network when it grows to a billion or 2 billion people and ... it literally changes your relationship with society, with each other ... It probably interferes with productivity in weird ways. God only knows what it's doing to our children's brains."
(End of article)

79

It's been said that it's easier to fool people than to convince them that they have been fooled. This holds today. After hearing these comments, I realized and recognized the power of this manipulation.

Maturity is hindered in an individual's life because of a strong desire to be the center of attention, even if it's artificial. The growth process is stunted, leaving individuals vulnerable to false and deceitful information. This psychological manipulation is released to the public for the sole purpose of financial gain. I can only imagine social media and its effect in the decades to come.

The persuasion of a Prophet comes from trust. Real or false, when the hearers trust the medium or media like sheep, they will follow. We see our communications devices as neutral. We don't expect our various apps, social media platforms, and devices to have a plan.

January 11th, 2018, and an investigative report by Project Veritas ∠ Twitter Engineers To "Ban a Way of Talking" Through "Shadow Banning,"

On January 3rd, 2018, at a San Francisco restaurant, Abhinav Vadrevu, a former Twitter Software Engineer, explains a strategy called "shadow banning," that to his knowledge, Twitter has employed: "One strategy is to shadow ban, so you have ultimate control. The idea of a shadow ban is that you ban someone, but they don't know they've been banned, because they keep posting and no one sees their content. So they just think that no one is engaging with their content, when in reality, no one is seeing it."

Twitter is in the process of automating censorship and banning, says Twitter Software Engineer Steven Pierre on December 8th of 2017:

"Every single conversation is going to be rated by a machine and the machine is going to say whether or not it's a positive thing or a negative thing. And whether it's positive or negative doesn't

(inaudible), it's more like if somebody's being aggressive or not. Right? Somebody's just cursing at somebody, whatever, whatever. They may have a point, but it will just vanish... It's not going to ban the mindset; it's going to ban, like, a way of talking."

Former Twitter Engineer Conrado Miranda confirms on December 1st, 2017, that tools are already in place to censor pro-Trump or conservative content on the platform.

When asked whether or not these capabilities exist, Miranda says, "that's a thing."

In a conversation with former Twitter Content Review Agent Mo Norai on May 16th, 2017, we learned that in the past, Twitter would manually ban or censor Pro-Trump or conservative content. When asked about the process of banning accounts, Norai said, "On stuff like that it was more discretion on your viewpoint, I guess how you felt about a particular matter..."

When asked to clarify if that process was automated, Norai confirmed that it was not: "Yeah, if they said this is: 'Pro-Trump' I don't want it because it offends me, this, that. And I say I banned this whole thing, and it goes over here and they are like, 'Oh you know what? I don't like it too. You know what? Mo's right, let's go, let's carry on, what's next?'"

Norai also revealed that more left-leaning content would go through their selection process with less political scrutiny, "It would come through checked and then I would be like 'Oh you know what? This is okay. Let it go.'"

Norai explains that this selection process wasn't exactly Twitter policy, but instead, they were following unwritten rules from the top: (End of article)

I've watched families divided, and friends become enemies because someone left out a critical piece of information. I've watched good people do bad things thinking they were justified to find out later they didn't have the whole story. To leave out important information or to slant news is to deceive. It is the very art of deception. The Nations of the false prophet will condition people to accept certain information without question. The people will trust the media or medium the information comes through.

In summary, these nations are nations of great technology. We have a kingdom of two nations that are world powers during the time of the beast. They are masters at propaganda. They look <u>CHRIST LIKE but speak like devils</u>. (Mth.15v18). They promote the first beast and give power to his image that it might be worshiped. They are united and <u>have the technology to institute a worldwide identification system.</u> They have power over the world economies. What nations could fit this bill? The Bible calls them THE FALSE PROPHET.Rev.19v20,,13v14.

So, we have the European Union and a union of two powerful nations that fly the flag of Christianity. One crucial point about the northern alliance is **it looks Christian,** though it's false.

Rev 18:3 For all nations have drunk of the wine of the wrath of her fornication, and the kings of the earth have committed fornication with her, and the merchants of the earth are waxed rich through the abundance of her delicacies. 4 And I heard another voice from Heaven, saying, **Come out of her, my people, that ye be not partakers of her sins,** and that ye receive not of her plagues.

Rev 17:6 And I saw the woman drunken with the blood of the saints, and with the blood of the martyrs of Jesus: and when I saw her, I wondered with great admiration.

Speculation: I believe the False Prophet will be the United States and either Canada or Britain.

I strongly favor Britain and the United States.

When you look at Britain's long history of murdering the citizens of nations for their resources like South Africa and India under colonialism, or the United States record of destroying the unity of nations through bloodshed for the profit of a big business, you can't help seeing these nations as a beast. At the same time, both nations have a solid Christian background. They have sent more missions than all the other nations combined. I believe we will see a future alliance with two of these nations.

THE TEN KINGS

Kings with No Kingdom

The Bible shows us at least ten neutral nations in this conflict before they join the beast.

Rev 17:12 And the ten horns which thou sawest are ten kings, which **have received no kingdom as yet;** but receive power as kings one hour with the beast. 13 These have one mind, and **shall give their power and strength unto the beast.** 14 These shall make war with the lamb, and the lamb shall overcome them: for he is Lord of lords, and king of kings: and they that are with him are called, and chosen, and faithful. Rev 17:16 And the ten horns which thou sawest upon the beast, **these shall hate the whore,** and shall make her desolate and naked, and shall eat her flesh, and burn her with fire. 17 For God hath put in their hearts to fulfil his will,

From this text, we know that these represent ten nations not part of the European Union, nor the nations of the false prophet. They don't belong to the opposition forces, King of the South. Receiving power for one hour is symbolic of a brief season or period.

John 4:21 Jesus saith unto her, woman, believe me, the hour cometh, when ye shall neither in this mountain, nor yet at Jerusalem, worship the Father.

Luke 22:53 When I was daily with you in the temple, ye stretched forth no hands against me: but this is your hour, and the power of darkness.

One interesting question about these future kings is from where do their kingdoms come? If they were appointed rulers over conquered lands, there would be no need for political and military allegiance (Power and Strength) to the beast. He would already have it. The scriptures say it's their power and strength, not the beast. So, are we witnessing ten separate coups where these men are instated and then turn over control and strength? This exchange of power, instant rule, for all ten nations happens in the same hour, which implies the same time, and it is made clear they "receive power." In Greek text, this means to take hold. This is an opportunity they seize.

This opportunity is given to them, but it's not clear by whom. This also raises the question, who did they replace? Another problem with the coup theory is they have one mind. They are unified in thinking and work together even in their hatred and destruction of the harlot. They're working independently of the beast's kingdom and make war with the Lamb.

What we see in Revelation Chapter 17 are ten leaders who have access to nations and take leadership over those nations for a season with the beast. They are somehow connected, and they fight in unison.

Speculation. This could be a NATO or UN-type organization. To illustrate their power, on March 8th, 2012, secretary of defense Leon Panetta gave the American people a startling revelation. While addressing Congress concerning actions in Syria,

He was asked where he received authority to deploy U.S. troops in a foreign conflict. His response was the United Nations. He stated the UN preempts congressional authority on some military actions concerning America's military. Article I, Section 8, Clause 11 of the U.S. Constitution grants Congress the power to declare war. The U.S. President then directs the actions of the military as Commander and Chief. Somewhere along the line, our constitution has been sidestepped and overlooked. The UN challenges the sovereignty of Nations. This is only a prelude of what is to come.

THE UPRIGHT ONES

When the Sixth King of the North enters Israel after conquering the king of the south, he comes with an ally.

This ally is called the Upright One in Dan 11:17. The Hebrew word is "yashar." It means just, upright, equity, and straight. Who are they? Possibly the ten horns of Revelation chapter 17, it's not made clear. We know they are a group with Military Power because this verse is about military occupation.

It's important to see they're siding with the beast at this point of the conflict.

Speculation: This seems like an alliance of nations the beast uses for political favor in his entrance to Israel. This is possibly the ten nations or their organization before their ascension to join him.

The last Days Line up.

The King of the South & Allies	The King of North & Allies
Dan. 11:5	**Dan. 9: 26 & 11:4-17**
Turkey	European Union
Egypt	The Upright Ones

ALL THE PLAYERS

Ezek. 30:5	**Rev. 13 & Rev.17:11-14**
Egypt	European Union
Men of League.	False Prophet
Ethiopia	Ten Kings
Lydia = Turkey	*
Mingled People /Arabia	*
Chub (N African Nation)	*

CHAPTER 5)

THE WARS & RUMORS OF WARS

Interpreting tool

What do words mean? The Greek words "allos" and "heteros" are usually translated as "another" in English, yet "allos" literally means "another of the same type or similar" and "heteros" means "another of a different or opposite type." The languages the Bible is interpreted from are more complex than our English.

A WORLD IN CHAOS

Mat 24:6 And ye shall hear of wars and rumors of wars: see that ye be not troubled: for all these things must come to pass, but the end is not yet.:7 For nation shall rise against nation, and kingdom against kingdom: and there shall be famines, and pestilences, and earthquakes, in divers places.:8 All these are the beginning of sorrows.

The word for nations in the Greek language is "tribe." The word kingdom would be described today as nations. It means realm or reign. The same word used in...

Rev 11:15 And the seventh angel sounded; and there were great voices in heaven, saying, The **kingdoms** of this world are become the kingdoms of our Lord, and of his Christ; ...

These conflicts will be tribe against tribe and nation against nation. We see that today because the beginning of sorrows has begun. From South Africa to the shores of Korea, Tribalism is alive and well in the twenty-first century. Ethnic, racial, and religious disagreements are festering into a violent whirlwind of death and desolation worldwide, leaving countless souls homeless and nationless. Yemen battles of Saudi Arabia and the Houthis have leftover ten thousand dead. The Iraqi Kurds and the Islamic States battle for Mosul led to over forty thousand civilian deaths in 2017 alone. This is not counting military casualties. Syria with the Jihadi groups versus the Islamic State, leaving over a quarter million Syrian's dead and Millions of Syrians fleeing their homeland. Egypt and ISIL terror attacks; Nigeria, Chad, and Cameron's clashes with Boko Haram. North and South Sudan, Israel and the Palestinians, Columbia, Afghanistan, Turkey, and the list go on and on. This is just from 2017.

Then there are the "rumors." The word for rumors in Mathew chapter twenty-four is the Greek word "akoe." Unlike the English definition that means unsubstantiated report, it means a report that's being popularized or that stands out. Something said or reported that gains an audience. **The same word is often used as fame in the New Testament**. *(Mark 1:28, Mat 14:1, Mat 4:24)*

These are the rumors of wars that gain worldwide attention. We see that today. South Korea versus North Korea is a conflict that will have international consequences and will possibly involve world superpowers especially considering the constant saber-rattling of North Korea towards the south's central alley, the United States. Two nations with nuclear capabilities that still have minor skirmishes on their border are India and Pakistan. The tension between Iran and Saudi Arabia has reached a fever pitch, and rumors are flying of military conflict. In Iraq, we hear whispers of civil war as the Kurds seek independence. Then there's China versus the U.S. over the South China Sea, North Korea versus the U.S. on sanctions and Missile testing, Russia vs. the U.S. based on lies and accusations of espionage. All three nations are supporting smaller nations with a vested interest at odds with one another. The Bible says this is just the warmup for what's about to come.

Mat 24:8 All these are the beginning of sorrows. (The beginning of birth pains)

THE FORMING OF ALLIANCES

We define the word alliance: a union or association **formed for mutual benefit**, especially between countries or organizations; a relationship based on an affinity in interests, nature, or qualities. It's the state of being joined or associated. It's time to look at these nations and find the strings that tie them together for the end-time conflict.

THE NORTHERN ALLIANCES /WHAT GLUES THEM TOGETHER

In 1950, the **European** Coal and Steel Community began to unite **European** countries economically and politically. The six founding countries are Belgium, France, Germany, Italy, Luxembourg, and the Netherlands. **On March 25, 1957**, they signed a treaty in Rome establishing the European Economic Community (E.E.C.), which by 1993 became the (E.C.), Economic Community and the nations identified them as the European Union. The nations that once represented the Roman Empire had reemerged. The beast of Revelation chapter 13 had begun to breathe.

It's important to understand that in the book of Revelation, we receive a world view of all the countries and nations on the planet from heaven's perspective. God sees these nations as a beast; as terrible creatures that are evil, violent, and the worst influence on the earth, nations chosen by the devil. Through these nations, he will work terrible things. Though the anti-Christ is not yet in power, the spirit of anti-Christ is becoming more prevalent, especially in the nations of his alliance. Worst of all, these beasts cloak themselves with the banner of Christianity.

Anti-Christ 1 John 2:18 Little children, it is the last time: and as ye have heard that antichrist shall come, even now are there many antichrists; whereby we know that it is the last time.

The Greek word for anti-Christ is "antichristos," meaning the opponent of Christ. Remember, Christ is the anointed one from God, the Messiah. The beast opposes the true and living God.

He opposes all that is true. Understanding this spirit helps us understand what's happening in the nations around us and the spirit that unifies them, what causes them to become "Birds of a feather...." We don't have the identities of the False Prophet, but the Bible clarifies that they would have the same spirit. (Rev 16:13) **Note the attributes and commonalities** of the beast in the scriptures.

Little Horn Dan 7:25 And he shall speak great words against the most High, and shall wear out the saints of the Most High, and think to change times and laws: and they shall be given into his hand until a time and times and the dividing of time.

The Vile One Dan 11:36 "Then the king shall do according to his own will: he shall exalt and magnify himself above every god, shall speak blasphemies against the God of gods, and shall prosper till the wrath has been accomplished; for what has been determined shall be done. :37 "He shall regard neither the God of his fathers nor the desire of women, nor regard any god; for he shall exalt himself above them all. :38 "But in their place he shall honor a god of fortresses; and a god which his fathers did not know he shall honor with gold and silver, with precious stones and pleasant things.

Son of Destruction 2 Th 2:3 Let no man deceive you by any means: for that day shall not come, except there come a falling away first, and that man of sin be revealed, the son of perdition; 4 Who opposeth and exalteth himself above all that is called God, or that is worshipped; so that he as God sitteth in the temple of God, showing himself that he is God.

Rev 13:4 And <u>they worshipped the dragon</u> which gave power unto the beast: <u>and they worshipped the beast</u>, saying, Who is like unto the beast? who is able to make war with him? 5 <u>And there was given unto him a mouth speaking great things and blasphemies; and power was given unto him to continue forty and two months.</u> :6 <u>And he opened his mouth in blasphemy against God, to blaspheme his name, and his tabernacle, and them that dwell in heaven.</u> 7 And it was given unto him to make war with the saints, and to overcome them: and power was given him over all kindreds, and tongues, and nations. :8 <u>And all that dwell upon the earth shall worship him, whose names are not written in the book of life</u> of the Lamb slain from the foundation of the world.

The hard truth about all these beast descriptions is that they all describe Western cultural elements. If you study modern western culture, you will find it comes down to the influence of two nations, the United States and Europe, with its roots arising from ancient Greece.

The original definition will say it's based on Judeo-Christian values. This was true. Over time, the democracy and freedoms we fought for have evolved and taken on a different meaning, from the freedom to live and do what's right for the whole to the freedom to do what I want. The pursuit of what is honorable has morphed into the pursuit of what is pleasurable and popular. We celebrate the proud and arrogant. It's fashionable to attack all values Christian and Hebrew. These are the images broadcast worldwide and have affected almost every nation on the planet. Look at the beast's actions compared to what we already see in developed western societies. We will see where they're headed.

The new cultural norm is the isolation and persecution of Christianity. The same source of values the culture is based on. All the western nations have what's described as a Christian Heritage.

I was recently reading a biography of someone who lived during the 1930s in the U.S. What struck me was the comment that to have sexual intercourse outside of marriage was considered a sign of mental illness. This was a national mindset at the time. It doesn't mean it didn't occur, but there was a powerful scriptural influence on the majority.

Even Adolph Hitler hid his mistress Eva Braun from camera view until he could justify her presence because he feared public opinion. Affairs were not acceptable at the time. Not even from their beloved Fuhrer. They understood the strength of family and society is marriage.

The challenge we face today is what western culture once represented and what it has evolved into today—two different cultures. Christianity does not fit the current. Christianity **is its own culture**. It's a culture of conversion and transformation. It cannot be mixed; it doesn't conform and is often viewed by this generation as intolerant. Therefore, as society moves toward Christian culture, it is easily digested. When a society moves away from Christian culture, Christianity becomes a hindrance. These nations will be hostile towards true Christianity. I say true Christianity because outside of the Harlot that rides the beast, they won't be aggressive towards certain forms of Christianity. Those that hold a modern, more philosophical secular view of the scriptures. Faith that doesn't lead to action will be embraced. Speaking of the last days, in 2nd Timothy chapter 3, Paul says this about the apostate end times church, *"Having a form of godliness, but denying the power thereof:....."* Biblical values are being attacked and removed from the societal structure.

For many years, we have seen this in the United States, Europe, and other western nations, where Christianity once thrived. Today we see an accelerating of this values clash happening in the European Union.

In an article from Powerline July 9, *2017, by Paul Mirengoff Titled Europe's Childless Leaders. James McPherson, writing in the Washington Examiner,* makes a remarkable observation, **the leaders of Europe have no children:**

"...France's Emmanuel Macron has none. Same with German Chancellor Angela Merkel, British prime minister Theresa May, Italian prime minister Paolo Gentilon, Holland's Mark Rutte, Scotland's Nicola Sturgeon, and Jean-Claude Juncker, President of the European Commission. Sweden's prime minister Stefan Lofven has no biological children.

The prime minister of Luxembourg is also childless. I mention him not to cherry-pick, but because it means that of the six founding members of what evolved into the European Union, five are now led by childless prime ministers or presidents. As George Weigel says, this would have been unimaginable to one of the founders of modern "Europe," Konrad Adenauer, who was the father of eight." (End of article)

This is a culture that devalues family. Self should always be preeminent. The family will be an experiment to be <u>redefined</u> by the pleasures of men.

Today there's a great temptation to compromise spiritually. The great attack on Christian values has caused many denominations and organizations to unify, strength in numbers. The problem is doctrine divides. It's meant to.

Most of what divides the church is minor in light of forwarding the kingdom of God, our overall mission.

Unity at all costs is not possible. The Bible makes clear the doctrinal deal breakers are Idolatry and sexual immorality. This was well established in the early church. As we are hurled towards the last days, you will find an acceptance of these belief systems instead of a calling out and separation from them. (Rev 2:14, Rev 2:20)

He shall not desire women. *(Dan 11:37)* The Hebrew word "chemdah" used throughout Old Testament implies attraction. He will not be attracted to women. Many believe he will be Homosexual. That is a strong probability. In any case, this is a true mark of western culture. The anti-Christ will be a deviant; the world applauds going against all that is natural in human sexuality. I can write a separate book on what the Bible describes as the decadence of the last days. Open sexual perversion will play a huge part in these alliances. It is western culture that promotes the LGBT lifestyle under the guise of tolerance. Western culture fosters abortion under the deceptive title freedom of choice, and it is the culture of the West that attacks the core of what holds societies together, marriage. This will be one of the reasons many nations will oppose him, especially those belonging to Islam.

The word fortress is used 39 times in Hebrew, most often used as strong or strength. He Honors military might and will honor it with materialism. *(Gold and precious things)* He will reward aggression and conquest.

Finally, this will be a generation that worships Satan. They will also worship the beast. It's important to note God separates them, the worship of Satan from the beast. Dragon (Satan) worship is hedonism. (Rev 13:4,8)

The word comes from the Greek word for pleasure. The emphasis is on self. **What we can expect is hedonism dressed in the appearance of Christianity.** This worship is about **lifestyle**. A popular word that describes the youth of this generation is narcissism. In his book, *Freedom to Learn, Peter Gray Ph.D. says:*

"Narcissism is a serious social and psychological problem. The term refers to an inflated view of the self, coupled with relative indifference to others. People who are high in this trait fail to help others unless there is immediate gain or recognition to themselves for doing so; often think they are above the law and therefore violate it; and readily trample over others in their efforts to rise to the "top," which is where they think they belong. A world full of narcissists would be a sad world indeed."
(End of article)

This will be the culture of that generation. The worship of Satan will be a generational mindset.

Satan worship is the worship of self. **Self-idolization.** The beast will be their rock star. He will be the embodiment of all they desire, the icon of what they want to be. **He will be their idol.** We even see this on the world political stage today.

July 3, 2017. REUTERS Reported on French President Emmanuel Macron's speech at a special congress gathering both houses of parliament (National Assembly and Senate) at the Versailles Palace, near Paris. Macron himself has said he plans a "Jupiterian" presidency - as a remote, dignified figure, **like the Roman God of gods**, who weighs his rare pronouncement carefully.

Narcissism incarnate, welcome to the new age. Like all Icons, the world will blindly worship the beast, following his lead down the road that leads to Destruction. Western culture is his song. It's the medium that spreads his spirit. **This will be an ideology of all his allies, the nations of the False Prophet, The Ten Kings, and The Upright Ones.**

THE SOUTHERN ALLIANCES /WHAT GLUES THEM TOGETHER

Dan 11:7 But out of a branch of her roots shall one stand up in his estate, which shall come with an army, and shall enter into the fortress of the king of the north, and shall deal against them, and shall prevail.

The only root of Arsinoe II is Ptolemy (Epigone) of Telmessos, an ancient city of Turkey. The great king of the south arises. Unlike the King of the North, the king of the south and his allies are more clearly identified in scripture.

Today in the Middle East, one great power that is rarely recognized and often underestimated is Turkey. The nation of Turkey, as of 2018, has the eight most powerful military on the planet. Its standing army is larger than Germany and France's armies combined. Its navy is almost twice the size of Great Britain's, and its population is double the size of Russia. Turkey boasts the world's 19th largest nominal G.D.P. Turkey is sometimes referred to as the cradle of civilization. The Tigris and Euphrates rivers flow from it, leading some to believe the Garden of Eden was located there. This is where God settle Noah's Arch on Mt. Ararat.

Humanity's second chance flowed from this territory. This is the location for the seven gentile churches of Revelation. The irony is today, the nation of Turkey is 98% Islamic. The Ottoman Turks overran the Byzantine Empire in 1453 A.D. Later, Turkey, Syria, Palestine, and by 1517 Egypt fell. By 1683 the Ottoman Turks had spread their empire into Europe, Asia, and Africa. From the Caucasus Mountains to the Persian Gulf and the Islands of the eastern Mediterranean, all fell to the Ottoman Turks. The Turkish empire fell after the First World War, and the Turkish people were left with the region we know today as Turkey. The rest of their empire was divided between the Arabs that fought against them and are the nations that make up the Middle East today. If Turkish history proves one thing, it is from the beginning of the great Ottoman Empire until today, they have learned to adapt to change.

Turkey began to modernize and build after WWII–a war in which they did not participate. They formed a relationship with a new ally, the United States. This relationship neutralized the threat of their archenemy Russia. Through economic and military aid from the U.S. and the brilliance of Turkish leadership, today, Turkey stands as one of the most powerful military powers in the Middle East.

Turkey will lead the Middle East. They will do it in the spirit of Islamic Culture as the heart of this culture is Sharia Law. It is the compiled code and laws governing the life and behavior of Muslims.

It affects Muslim traditions, views of justice, economics, and politics. Sharia Law creates culture. It's important to understand that, for almost a century, Turkey was considered secular. Under their law, all religions were equal. Though there were few Jews or Christians, this applied to all, especially the sects of Islam and secularists. This was enforced by its military, which, unlike most nations, operated outside the government. This was the people's checks and balances for a possible tyrannical government. Through political manipulation, this has changed, and one sect now has overall influence. The Southern alliances are birds of a feather also, the bird being Sunni Muslim.

An example of Islamic culture is summarized in a *Huffington Post Article from World Post by Nikolas Kozloff concerning Turkey's Prime Minister, Recep Tayyip Erdogan.*

"Despite such differences, the protests seem to underscore a certain degree of disenchantment if not outright hostility toward

Prime Minister Recep Tayyip Erdogan's increasingly Islamist tendencies. Many protesters at Taksim have displayed portraits and photos of Mustafa Kemal Ataturk, the father of Turkey's secular state. For years, Erdogan's so-called "moderate" Islamist-rooted Justice and Development Party or A.K.P. has sought to impose Muslim values on society.

Indeed, even before becoming prime minister, Erdogan railed that "one cannot be a Muslim and secular. **For them to exist together is not a possibility."** While serving as Mayor of Istanbul, Erdogan also remarked that he was "a servant of Shari'a" and "the imam of Istanbul."

Later, once ensconced in power as prime minister, Erdogan used public funds to construct 17,000 mosques while announcing plans to build a super mosque overlooking Istanbul. The government proclaimed that every shopping mall, theater, or public facility in Turkey should sport a Muslim prayer room. Erdogan then decried the use of social media as "anti-Islam."

In an echo of the recent scandal at the National Security Agency and furor over whistle-blower Edward Snowden, Turkish intelligence has reportedly collected information about the religious affiliations of hundreds of individuals and companies, as well as figures close to the C.H.P. in order to prevent people from acquiring choice jobs in the public sector.

Welcome to A.K.P. Homophobia and Misogyny

In addition, the Erdogan government introduced Koran classes for primary school students and revived clerical training for middle school. Moreover, Erdogan ordered the separation of girls and boys in primary and secondary school and ridiculously ruled that tens of thousands of graduates of Islamic madrassas possess the equivalent of a college degree and therefore can be hired for high-level civil service posts. The government announced it would select two-thirds of the Turkish Academy of Sciences' members in a further blow to higher learning. Up until that point, existing members had been in charge of choosing recruits, and following the A.K.P.'s ruling, a full one-third of the Academy resigned in protest.

Next, Erdogan sought to roll back Turkey's modern social sphere by speaking out against gay rights. When the A.K.P. sought to criminalize adultery, the public grew even more nervous, and following severe criticism from the European Union, Erdogan was forced to back off. However, the prime minister advocates the separation of the sexes on beaches and wants subway passengers to refrain from kissing in public. Furthermore, to keep women in the home, Erdogan has opposed daycare centers but argues that all Turkish women should have three children. Meanwhile, Erdogan supports policies to compel women to adopt conservative dress and customs. Still, the misogynistic prime minister turns a blind eye to Turkey's backward child-bride practices and domestic violence. Moreover, Erdogan is against abortion and supports legislation reducing Turkey's legal abortion limit from 16 to 10 weeks. The prime minister says he even opposes abortion in cases of rape.

What inflamed public opinion, however, was Erdogan's move to ban the sale of alcohol between 10 p.m. and 6 a.m. and to prohibit sales near schools and mosques furthermore. When Erdogan prohibited alcohol brands from advertising on T.V., billboards, and sporting events, some began to suspect that the A.K.P. had a stealth plan to abolish alcohol consumption altogether. When criticism began to mount that the new restrictions infringed on personal freedoms, Erdogan responded flippantly that "anyone who drinks is an alcoholic, save those who vote for A.K.P." Erdogan has taunted his opponents, remarking that if people want to drink, they should purchase ayran, a traditional yogurt drink, or alternatively eat grapes."

(End of article)

These cultural changes in Turkey's once secular society have already gained the approval of many Middle Eastern nations.

The next powerful ally of the King of The South is Egypt.

Egypt is one of the oldest civilizations in recorded history. On the northeastern part of the African continent, Egypt is a prominent player in bible prophecy. Today Egypt is a nation of over 93 million people, the largest Arab nation in the world. Over 90% of this population is Sunni Muslim. It has one of the largest militaries in the region, boosting troop strength of over a million active and reserve men, over 1100 aircraft, 4100 tanks, almost 14,000 armored vehicles, and 319 naval assets. Though it has a strong Military, Egypt suffers from a weak economy. The average wage is only $15,000 a year, and 25% of their population lives on about $27 a month. Egypt is not an official ally of Turkey today, but it will be soon.

Ethiopia

Ethiopia, once surrounded by the second river flowing from the Garden of Eden, Gihon, and recognized for the gemstones of topaz. Ethiopia has survived the turbulent challenges of time. What's impressive in scripture is that you see Ethiopia constantly matched with Egypt.... Isa 20:5 Nahum 3:9, Psa 68:31. Many ancient Historians tell us Ethiopia was the birthplace of Egypt. The Egyptians were Ethiopians who migrated to the coast. Later, to be dominated and replaced by other nationalities. Today Modern Ethiopia is a developing nation of over one hundred million people. Its military's personnel are about 162,000. The Sunni Muslims make up 33% of the population, second to the Ethiopian Orthodox Church.

Chub

The nation of Chub is only mentioned once in the scriptures. The historical evidence on its location is vague. The Hebrew word "kub" is defined as a country near Egypt: --Chub. That's our biggest hint, possibly Algeria or Tunisia to the West.

In any case, it's a nation not previously listed that is close to the nation of Egypt, somewhere in North Africa.

The Mingled People /Saudi Arabia

The word for mingled people means (transverse threads of cloth); also a mixture, (or mongrel race):--Arabia. This would have been the perfect picture of the Arabian people in Ezekiel's time. The ancient Arabians, or Arabes as the Hellenes called them, were Semitic people. One must note that the Arabians were not just a single people but divided into smaller kingdoms and tribes. One famous being Saba, or referred to in the Old Testament as Sheba, the home to great city builders and nomads. The Arabian People in this time were very successful at trade. The Nile and Euphrates gave them excellent access to other nations, which made them wealthy people. *(They once had colonies on both coasts of the Red Sea)* Today Saudi Arabia is still a trade king as the world's largest oil producer with the second-largest oil reserves. Saudi Arabia is the only Arab country to be part of the G20 major economies. The military spending of this economic power is eight times that of Egypt, yet its military is less than a third of their size.

Libya

Libya, decedents of the Berbers, was known as ancient Phoenicia during the time of Ezekiel, its greatest city being Carthage. Libya's Islamic roots began under the Ottoman Empire. After being conquered by the Persians, Greeks, Romans, Ottomans, Italians, and finally the allies of WWII, Libya was granted independence on December 24, 1951. A large oil reserve was discovered in 1959, and this developing nation became a wealthy state. This was also the beginning of many internal conflicts with her neighbors that climaxed with a civil war in 2011.

It was initiated by what's been called the Arab Spring. Today Libya is an unstable, poor nation with three rival governments fighting for control. Out of its population of six million people, 96% are Sunni Muslims.

Men of the League

'This Group speaks of a covenant or alliance with Egypt that is not given ancient geographical designation. It's important to remember Ezekiel chapter 30 is about the judgment of Egypt and its allies. They're not referred to as a nation but an individual group. These nations are military allies, so that would communicate this group of men have military power and influence.

Speculation. When I began to search for such a group that would be connected or could connect with all these nations, it wasn't hard to find, **The Muslim Brotherhood**. This political group began in 1928 in Egypt. They call themselves Transnational Sunni Islamists. Today they are the most prominent political organizations in Egypt. Their goal is to implement Sharia Law into Government. It started with the Government of Egypt. In 2012, their first Presidential candidate elected Mohamed Morsi, who was responsible for the crucifixion of Coptic Christians to trees, called themselves the Freedom and Justice Party.

This organization today has headquarters in Cairo, Egypt, Sudan, Afghanistan, Iraq, and Bahrain. In 1977 imprisoned members of the brotherhood released by Egyptian President Anwar Sadat formed a military wing, joining Al Gama'a Al Islamiyya.

105

Its Ideology is in harmony with many militant terrorists. Terrorist organizations founded by **members of the Muslim brotherhood** are **Hamas** (Hassan Al Banna), **Al Qaeda** (Osama Bin Laden), **ISIS**, his disciple (Abu Musab al-Zarqawi), and **Islamic Jahad** (Ayman al Zawahiri). Here, we see military elements unattached to any nation, connected by a political Ideology and a covenant to make Sharia the law of the world.

There's a tremendous ideological and theological difference between the two main sects of Islam. That's because, in Islam, theology and politics go hand in hand. The main dispute is about the succession of leadership. Shias believe that God must choose Muhammad's successor. They believe Muhammad divinely ordained his cousin and son-in-law Ali Ibn Abi Talib to led. Ali and his successors through bloodlines are called Imams. (Not to be confused with those who lead prayers at Mosque.) The largest Shia population in Iran. Shias make up over 90% of its population of 70 million.

Sunnis believe that Abu Bakr, the father of Muhammad's wife Aisha, was Muhammad's rightful successor. Sunnis believe the method of choosing or electing leaders guided by the Quran is the Muslim Community.

The next major issue is the Hadith. There are two significant sources of information for Muslims: the Holy Qur'an, on which all Muslims agree, and the Sunnah or Hadith, which includes the words, actions, and confirmations of the Prophet. Because they differ on a successor, they also have different books on the Hadith, which affects their view of Sharia law.

Summary

What we see in the southern alliance is a group of nations linked by a religious belief system.

Another interesting note is these nations have made military alliances. These agreements have already begun. Turkey and Greece have long-standing contentions and recently over maritime boundaries. Greece, representative of the Northern Kingdom, and Turkey representative of the south, are disputing drilling rights in the Mediterranean Sea. What's impressive is a nation in the center of this dispute is also a nation mentioned several times in prophecy concerning the last day's events. The nation of Cypress. The Island of Cypress is ethically divided, Half Greek and the other half Turkish. The dispute is over drilling rights for oil and natural gas. Notice the pattern of alliances being formed. In 2019, Turkey signed a maritime agreement with Libya. Later this agreement extended to military cooperation with Qatar & Libya, as Turkey is now establishing a military presence in Libya to aid in her current civil wars. Egypt opposed Turkey's move, but only on a political level. They resent Turkish support of the Muslim Brotherhood, Mohamed Morsi, who was removed by the Egyptian military after being elected President of Egypt. Turkey today is also the second-largest investor in Ethiopia. The pieces are moving into place.

THE NATION OF ISRAEL AND ALLIANCES

The whole focus of Daniel Chapter 11-12 is the Revelation of the plight of the Hebrew peoples in the last days. Mainly chapter eleven covers at least six years; I believe it covers all seven of the final years of Jewish destiny. After the Roman Legions sacked Jerusalem in 70 A.D. for 2000 years, the Jewish people would remain in exile. Then in a moment, after the heinous atrocities of the holocaust, they returned.

Isa 66:8 *Who hath heard such a thing? who hath seen such things? Shall the earth be made to bring forth in one day?*

*or **shall a nation be born at once?** for as soon as Zion travailed, she brought forth her children.*

What nation in history has ever gathered from the four corners of the planet to become a nation again; to resurrect a language that was dead, to be drawn to one place by a supernatural instinct like bees to honey, to call a place home that they have never known after centuries have passed?

I was not born to the WWII generation. I can't imagine the joy, the expectation, and the hope believers in Christ Jesus and Hebrews worldwide must have felt. One of the greatest and yet in their time, one of the impossible Biblical prophecies had come to pass.

Ezek 37:12 Therefore prophesy and say unto them, Thus saith the Lord G.O.D.; Behold, O my people, I will open your graves, and cause you to come up out of your graves, and bring you into the land of Israel.:13 And ye shall know that I am the LORD, when I have opened your graves, O my people, and brought you up out of your graves,:14 And shall put my spirit in you, and ye shall live, and I shall place you in your own land: then shall ye know that I the LORD have spoken it, and performed it, saith the LORD.

Daniel couldn't be present for Israel's May 14, 1948 declaration of independence, but I know he rejoiced. We know the Saints rejoiced on June 7, 1967, when Israel took back the ancient city of Jerusalem, God's Holy Hill. The supernatural hand of grace on this nation is like no other. From one conflict and crisis to the next, their survival has been described as inexplicable. We know God has stacked the deck.

Today, a generation later, the once weak fledgling nation of immigrants holds the third most stable economy globally, according to a report in 2016 published by the Bloomberg financial news agency. The United States is not ranked that high. The Israeli military is rank 18th worldwide by GFP, out of 138 nations. With 652 Aircraft, over 10,000 armored vehicles, and 2600 battle tanks, she has become a significant force in such a short time.

The question is, where does Israel stand in these future conflicts? Israel's population is made up of about seventy different nationalities. They come from all over the world, many not sharing the same language. Jewish culture is similar to American in that other cultures assimilate into one overall identity. They don't lose the culture of origin but take on the National Identity. Something Europe hasn't been able to accomplish. Religion is a powerful influence on Israeli culture. Judaism is Israel's official religion, and 74% of the country's inhabitants are Jewish, and about 90% speak Hebrew. 18% of the people in Israel are Arab Muslims, 2% are Christians, and 2% are Druze. (Ref. Jewishvirtuallibrary)

49% of Jewish Israelis are secular yet, a majority of Jews participate in the cultural practices of Judaism. It's taught in their school system. Though they are unique compared to many Middle Eastern nations, western culture has slowly made inroads. The Times of Israel reported an estimated 15,000 illegal abortions committed in a year. The LGBT community is growing, and religion in their education system is being challenged. The beast of western culture is rising in Israel.

Israel has diplomatic ties with 157 countries, but I wouldn't call these allies. Good relations for Israel historically come from nations where people identify with Jewish values and history. The U.S., Britain, Mexico and Canada, and the European Union are the strongest.

Israel has a formal peace treaty with Egypt and Jordan. What's clear in Daniel is that the E.U. will be an ally of Israel at that time.

Dan 11:16 -20 Reveals that when the north puts down the south, he shall also march into Israel. There is animosity between Europe and Israel, because the Bible says he consumes it. This is the Sixth King of the North. Israel is responsible for something awful. (Dan 11:14-17)

The Seventh King of the North has Israel paying reparations. Why pay reparations for fighting the same enemy? They did something that all sides disapproved of, and God in Daniel 11 names them" the robbers of thy people," meaning violent tyrants and destroyers. Another piece of evidence of the E.U. connection is with the Eight kings of the north. They enter into some agreement with him.

What's important to understand about Israel militarily in these times is Jerusalem. When God gave the children of Israel their inherited lands, Jerusalem was bordered by Judah and belonged to Benjamin. The Jebusites occupied Jerusalem, and though defeated by Joshua and eventually Judah (Judg 1:8), they were never wholly expelled from their stronghold in Zion.

Judge 1:21 And the children of Benjamin did not drive out the Jebusites that inhabited Jerusalem; but the Jebusites dwell with the children of Benjamin in Jerusalem unto this day.

2 Sam 5:7 Nevertheless David took the stronghold of Zion: the same is the city of David.

David defeated them and made Jerusalem a holy and royal city for all Israel. David established his throne and Judge Israel there. The Ark of the Covenant was brought there. God spoke these words about Jerusalem.

2 Chr 6:5 'Since the day that I brought My people out of the land of Egypt, I have chosen no city from any tribe of Israel in which to build a house, that My name might be there, nor did I choose any man to be a ruler over My people Israel. :6 'Yet I have chosen Jerusalem, **that My name may be there**; and I have chosen David to be over My people Israel.'

Jerusalem Is God's chosen city to be a witness of His name to the world. This geological location belongs to Him. It is set aside for His purpose. The people of Israel are His inheritance, but Jerusalem is His property. This is a fact the world cannot comprehend. God is not concerned about the size of armies, the geopolitical layout, or world opinion. God Almighty has set in motion His purposes, for this property, in these end times.

2 Chr 7:16 "For now I have chosen and sanctified this house, that My name may be there forever; and My eyes and My heart will be there perpetually. NKJV

Interpreting tool

This would be a **good time to speak on speculation**. Speculation is defined by the Oxford Dictionary: Forming a theory or conjecture without firm evidence.

Speculation can be helpful if we <u>make it clear this is our opinion and not Biblical fact</u>. Paul, the apostle, used this.

1 Cor 7:24-27 Brethren, let every man, wherein he is called, therein abide with God. :25 Now concerning virgins I have no commandment of the Lord: <u>yet I give my judgment</u>, as one that hath obtained mercy of the Lord to be faithful. :26 I suppose therefore that this is good for the **present distress,** I say, that it is good for a man so to be.:27 Art thou bound unto a wife? seek not to be loosed. Art thou loosed from a wife? seek not a wife.

Marriage is the will of God and an option for all believers. (Mat 19:5, Gen 2:24) The word judgment is the Greek word for advice/ opinion. Paul made it clear he had no scripture to draw from to make his point, but because of the conditions and pressures against this church's "present distress," he gave an opinion to help their understanding and deal with the decisions facing their situation. Speculation should never be its own truth but flow with existing truth. It should help illuminate what's already there. In this case, Paul was moving in the spirit of compassion and mercy. I will use this tool often in this book and do my best to separate it from scriptural evidence.

THINGS ARE ABOUT TO CHANGE

NATIONS AND THE BATTLES THAT ARE COMING

This is a list of other major players. I added a few previously mentioned nations only briefly for a complete picture. There will be many other nations in conflict during these final days.

The scriptures are vague on what wars take place before the final seven years. What they do reveal is the final alliances. I believe the seeds of tension have already been planted, and if we look closely and examine the scriptures, we can catch a glimpse of what's coming.

We can see the pieces moving in place. I believe these are the outcomes and confrontation we will witness until the 6th king of the North steps into view for the final seven years. The Bible is particular on what will happen in the order of those battles.

THE U.S. & EUROPE

The United States of America. /Creator of NATO and critical leader in the United Nations.

Today there is no military power on earth that can compare to The United States of America. Not China, neither Russia nor Europe. The U.S. has over 800 bases on foreign soil. They have over 400 naval assets. Their large naval fleets with modern nuclear capabilities are present on all seven seas. Unlike China with most of their naval assets boxed in the South China Sea.

The U.S. has close to 14,000 thousand aircraft, and this number doesn't include their Military Drone & Satellite capabilities. Russia has only about 4,000 aircraft. The U.S. has close to 6,000 combat tanks and over 41,000 armored fighting vehicles, not including artillery. Their 1,400,000 active-duty personnel have the most modern weapons and equipment to date. The U.S. has been in many conflicts. I'll start with WWII., the Korean war, 1950, Lebanon, 1957, Cuba, 1962, Vietnam War., 1964, 1970, Cambodia, Grenada, 1983, The Persian Gulf, Panama, Liberia, Iraq, Kuwait, Somalia, and the list goes on. The point is their military doctrine and experience are vast. It is **estimated** that the United States maintains an arsenal of over 6,800 nuclear bombs. Of those, more than 2,000 were deployed. That means 2000 nuclear warheads spread out on the seven seas are ready to be launched by aircraft bombers, aircraft carriers, battleships, cruisers, destroyers, and frigates. The United States also has the world's largest G.D.P. She can support her military.

In Revelation chapter 13, the Bible reveals a powerful revelation to us who live in these times. To many, it would seem improbable. The United States will no longer be the military leader of the world.

Rev 13:4 And they worshipped the dragon which gave power unto the beast: and they worshipped the beast, saying, Who is like unto the beast? Who is able to make war with him?

The word" able" in Greek is "dunamai," which means power. **Who has the power to war with the beast?** From the world's perspective, no other military could compare to that of the European Union.

Today the European Unions' military is disorganized at best. One of their greatest challenges is consolidating systems. Different countries mean different equipment and systems making unity difficult. Most nations have a common language, not Europe. It's the iron mixed with clay. If you include Great Britain, in 2017, the E.U. had four of the top militaries in the world. Britain the 6th, France 5th, Germany 9th and Italy 11th. Their combined militaries are only about 10% larger than the U.S. If you remove Britain, the combined are much smaller.

The U.S. spends double the amount on its military than all these, including Britain combined.

This tells me America's current standing will change. This could mean Europe will rise to be greater, or the U.S. will be diminished. Even if my speculation is correct and we are the False Prophet, we will stand in the shadow of Europe.

You might ask if it's the latter, how can the U.S. be diminished? One way is a strategy we've used on other nations to impede their growth, destabilization.

A perfect example of this is Iran 1979. The headlines read; Iranian militants seize the American Embassy in Tehran. In 1953 The U.S. and Britain helped overthrow the current Iranian democratically elected leader, Prime Minister Mohammad Mosaddegh, under operation code names "BOOT and TP-AJAX." Prime Minister Mosaddegh threatened Anglo Persian Oil companies (British Petroleum's) control over Iranian oil assets. They replaced him with Mohammad Reza Pahlavi, a loyalist and an oppressor who did little to help the plight of the impoverished Iranian people. In 1979 a rebellion led by Sayyid Ruhollah *Mūsavi* Khomeini, better known as

Ayatollah Khomeini, seized the embassy and recovered documents that proved U.S. involvement.

Iran was not the first or last nation we helped to overthrow or destabilize. On September 11, 1973, *the Presidential Palace of Chile was bombed* in a coup d'etat. Many didn't find out until years later that this was a C.I.A. funded operation executed to ensure the profits of an American Copper Manufacturer? In 1954 it was Guatemala after their first democratic elections for land owned by the United Fruit Company, a U.S. based business.

There are many more, 1948 French and Italian elections, 1958-63 Destabilization of Iraq, 1960-61 the Democratic Republic of Congo, 1959-63 failed attempts in Cuba, 1980-86 failed attempts in Nicaragua. These are only a few from our past *found online* in declassified C.I.A. documentation under the freedom of Information Act.

What I find interesting is the method we *employed* to destabilize these nations. In Iran, it started with a propaganda war. Accusations that the leader had communist affiliations and other slanders to produce distrust. Then they would hire thugs to commit mayhem.

The C.I.A. director in charge of the operation Kermit Roosevelt in an interview July 30, 1980, Los Angeles Times said ...

"He would have them surge through the streets of Tehran, break windows, beat up people, shoot their guns into mosques and shout, "We love Mossadegh. Up with Mossadegh and communism." And as if that wasn't enough, he then hired another mob to attack this mob to show that Tehran was in such chaos that anarchy was threatening and that to bring Iran back to a measure of stability, Mossadegh had to be overthrown," he says.

The strategy worked, and demonstrations escalated. Clashes broke out between opposing military factions. On August 19, 1953, anti-Mossadegh forces seized power, and Mossadegh went into hiding. An army general was installed as prime minister. The Shah made a triumphant return home."

This was the pattern used in many of our regime-change operations. Propaganda using media to plant seeds of division. The hiring of agitators to create civil unrest and, in some cases, whole militias for a justification for removal. Later they implemented infamous false flag operations.

Thus, creating a problem to be blamed on a targeted group for the sole purpose of executing a plan. We did this with bombs in Iran and C.I.A. bombing missions in Guatemala. (Operation PBSUCCESS)

Many believe today that civil war is a growing possibility in America. We can see paid agitators at work in various demonstrations around the country. Government trust is at an all-time low and with reason. Our officials are constantly caught selling out national interest to special interest. The propaganda machine (Mainstream Media) is in full force, pushing a "them against us" racially or ideological charged messages. The "Church Report" investigation, held by Congress in 1975, reveals this was common practice for the C.I.A. Please understand the C.I.A. was created to gather and analyze foreign intelligence.

The report covered C.I.A. ties with both foreign and domestic news media. Approximately 50 of the assets were individual American journalists or employees of U.S. media organizations.

About half are "accredited" by U.S. media organizations. They also used more than a dozen United States news organizations and commercial publishing houses. The C.I.A. created American media assets for political propaganda purposes.

Pulitzer Prize Co-Winner *Carl Bernstein in an article in Rolling Stone Magazine (October 20, 1977). "C.I.A. and the Media."* Brought to light C.I.A. ties within these networks, run by well-known liberals with pro-American big business and anti-Soviet views like William S. Paley (C.B.S.), Henry Luce (Time and Life), Arthur Hays Sulzberger (*The New York Times*), Alfred Friendly (managing editor of *The Washington Post*), Jerry O'Leary (The Washington Star), Hal Hendrix (*Miami News*), Barry Bingham, Sr. (Louisville Courier-Journal), James S. Copley (Copley News Services) and Joseph Harrison (The Christian Science Monitor).

What amazed me about the Church Report is that 28% of the C.I.A.'s COINTELPRO efforts aimed to weaken Groups and set members against each other. I highly recommend reading a copy of this report, especially Book III, section 4 propaganda. I also recommend research on the operation "Mockingbird." A vast portion of the population is blind to the powerful seen and unseen forces fighting against unity through the media.

The other obvious method the U.S. could be diminished by is a major war. This method flows with the scriptural narrative and seems to be an inescapable consequence in the last days. The scriptures tell us that conflicts will increase like birth pains. I believe the tensions are set for wars around the world, just not world war. That is yet to come. The cards are dealt, and the opponents are facing each other.

The United States will be center stage. For instance, according to Pew Research, American power and influence is the number one threat to the people of Turkey, which is also a NATO ally. It's not only Turkey; the study reveals America's power and influence concerns have grown from 2013 to 2017and is one of the most concerning issues of the thirty nations surveyed around the globe. Anti-Russian sentiment has been growing strong in the U.S. and Europe over the past few years. October 20, 2017, President Trump signed an executive order allowing the military to draft retired pilots. Preparations have begun.

Speculation: There will be a confrontation with the U.S. and Europe versus Russia and her allies. The U.S. and the E.U. will be victorious, but at a great cost.

European Union.

The E.U. will soon face an extraordinary crisis. It may be war or another challenge. The only thing that can unify its army is a crisis. A conflict will force the E.U. to change its military organization and how it is lead. Today the E.U. has seven decision-making bodies as compared to the three in the U.S.

The executive branch, the President of the European Commission, serves a term of 5 years. They have had twelve Presidents since their inception. *Jean-Claude Juncker* was the twelfth elected in 2014. **The Bible says there will be seven kings**. This tells us the head will have authority to rule. This also means a radical change in the E.U. Governing system. I believe when that happens, we will see the first of the seven leaders according to prophecy.

What's important to remember is the E.U. is not the beast until they are one. Until they have one army and someone to lead it. They have slowly become one since the uniting of their business interest in 1957. Decades later, they established their government, and by 1994 established a united currency.

They initiated the establishment of a <u>unified</u> military in 2017, their 60th Anniversary. There is more to come.

Many have suggested the total downfall of the E.U. in the distant future. Some of the world's top strategists see the E.U. in decline with no firm hopes of recovery. There are various economic reasons listed, but the main reason is its immigration policy and the rise of populism. They believe this will leave irreversible damage. This might be true. I have faith in the scriptures. The beast will rise, and the Catholic and Orthodox Church will be the church of the land. The mainstream media doesn't give much airtime to the revolution this Immigration policy has caused. What they call right-wing movements is a reviving of Europe's orthodox roots. This movement has permeated almost all Central and Eastern Europe. While Western Europe is fragmenting, Central and Eastern Europe are strengthening in nationalism. This spirit of nationalism is not just happening in Europe. It's a phenomenon that's happening worldwide. Nationalism isn't about skinheads and Nazis, as the propaganda in the media suggests. It's about Identity, National Identity. This desire for identity drives us toward our cultural roots, be it religion or racial pride.

In an article published on October 23, 2015, by Kaldaya called The Surprising Rise of Christianity in Russia.

A wave of revival rose in the Russian Orthodox Church in 2015. Many, including the Russian President, attributed the rise of patriotism to this. More Russians are attending church than at any time since WWII. In Japan, you have the Japanese President Shinzo Abe, who ran on a platform of returning Japan to its pre-WWII Glory. This is the battle cry for many up incoming right-wing nationalist groups who incorporate their religious beliefs like Shinto and Buddhism into their practices. In the Middle East, Turkey is an example.

The A.K.P.'s rise resulted from nationalism under Islam and the desire for Turkey to become a leader among Arab Muslim nations. This is the same spirit that has energized many of the radical Islamic Groups. You have Brexit, which was the exit of Brittan from the European Union. This was an issue of cultural identity and the return to traditional faith. Amazingly enough, traditional religion in Britain was in decline, but many right-wingers still claim Christianity as their faith. The New Church on the rise in Britain is the Evangelical church. President Donald Trump's win over Hillary Clinton was a political upset in every way. The world did not recognize the powerful right-wing national movement sweeping the country, a faith-based movement. This is what's happening in Europe.

European people are forsaking secularism and going back to their traditional roots. This is not like the revivals in China, where there are millions of conversions. This is about identity and tradition. This phenomenon goes beyond immigration. They are being drawn back to Orthodoxy. This is necessary for the fulfillment of prophecy. The E.U. made no place for religion in their constitution. This must change. The Bible tells us the Harlot rides the beast, meaning she will significantly influence the government. The E.U. will not disappear but rise unified with a harlot rider.

Even as Europe builds cohesiveness, there will always be instability. The iron is mixed with clay. On November 24, 2017, Poland passed a law forbidding businesses to operate on Sunday. This is a nation of almost 40 million people. It's a clear return to European religious roots.

Poland has banned immigration, and many European countries are looking to it as an example of a new Europe. The E.U. is right on course for their place in the end-time conflict.

THE MIDDLE EAST

There are wars and will be more wars in the Middle East. Today we see the conflicts within various Middle Eastern nations with various terrorist groups. The Shiite rebellion in Yemen, the battle with Isil in Iraq, the multi facade battles of Syria are but a few. Unity looks like a distant dream. The truth is most of these are proxy wars between Saudi Arabia and Iran and their ally's Russia and the United States. Since the end of WWII, the U.S. and Russia have fought to better position themselves militarily and economically on the world stage.

An example of this is when the U.S. rushed in to make Turkey and ally after WWII, and Russia rushed in to make Cuba and ally, after their revolution, to be closer to America's border. Because of Iran's hatred toward the western nations, they have partnered with Russia. This may be why they are not included as allies of Egypt in Ezekiel chapter 30 or their radical Shite stance against their neighbors. In any case, they have made themselves a target of many powerful nations. The U.S. has been a Saudi ally since the 1930s. The strife between Iran and Saudi Arabia is in part about money. The two have also historically been fierce oil competitors, but the strife goes much deeper.

In May 1981, the Saudi's formed the Gulf Cooperation Council **(G.C.C.), a** political and economic alliance of six Middle Eastern countries run by monarchs. Those nations are Saudi Arabia, Kuwait, The United Arab Emirates, Qatar, Bahrain, and Oman. The G.C.C. was established in Riyadh, Saudi Arabia.

The purpose of the G.C.C. is to achieve unity among its members based on their common objectives and similar political and cultural identities rooted in Islamic beliefs.

When Ayatollah Khomeini, a Shiite, came into power in 1979, he began calling for Islamic revolutions across the Muslim world. This became a direct threat to Iraq's secular leader Saddam Hussein whose nation held a Shite majority. Saudi Arabia also viewed this as potentially dangerous for the region, both financially with OPEC partners and even more for the region's Muslims. This conflict was not just about being Sunni or Shite. Both often pray in the same Mosque together. Iran's Shite leadership had accused the Sunni Royal family of being proxies for the West.

Then shortly after this was the Siege of Mecca, the same year where 100,000 worshipers were held hostage in Saudi Arabia's most sacred sites.

This was a great blow to the Islamic world. The seizure was led by Juhayman al-Otaybi, a member of an influential family in Najd (Saudi Arabia) who held the same sentiments that the Royal Family had sold out to the West. He was influenced by the Muslim Brotherhood and began his version (Ikhwan =brotherhood) in Saudi Arabia.

This was a significant blow to the Royal Family, especially since they experienced a rebellion of Shiites in the nation the same year. Then a Sunni member of their sect had committed the unthinkable to violate their most holy site and tradition.

The Saudis, after this point, no longer viewed the Muslim brotherhood in a neutral light. They considered the Iranian radical rhetoric dangerous to the whole region. The Saudis became a significant financier in the Iraq war against Iran and have been anti-Muslim brotherhood ever since, at least on the surface.

All the G.C.C. see the Muslim Brother Hood as a terrorist group except for Qatar. Qatar held a different view of the various Radical Islamic groups and gave haven to several, as Saudis had done with the Muslim brotherhood back in the '70s. The groups they have assisted are Al Qaeda, Hamas, the Muslim Brotherhood, and the Taliban. All these groups are Sunni Muslims. For this reason, Bahrain, Egypt, Libya, the Maldives, Saudi Arabia, the United Arab Emirates, and Yemen have severed relationships with Qatar. This is the first break in the G.C.C., and more importantly, this opens new allies for Qatar. Russia immediately swooped in and signed a defense agreement (even though the U.S. already has a large base there).

Iran re-established diplomatic relations, and Turkey signed an economic deal worth billions. Turkey also sent troops to aid Qatar and is setting up a military base in Qatar. Some believe they have their own vision for the Middle East.

Turkey is also pro-Muslim brotherhood; they share the same vision of a government run by Sharia Law. The scriptures make it clear. Turkey will lead, and the Saudi's will follow. Russia and Iran were not in that alliance. America will be pushed out of Qatar and out of the Middle East.

Speculation. The thing that separates the Middle East will be the same thing that unites it.

There will be a strong nationalist pull in these nations for governments to be run by Sharia Law. The leaders and Monarchs that resist will be overthrown. Somehow, Turkey will be the unifying factor. Turkey may be the deciding military factor in some of these nations. As Turkey ascends, I believe she will make Istanbul her capital again. Groups like the Muslim Brotherhood will increase in power.

CHINA & INDIA

Dan 11:44 But tidings out of the east.

The word "east" means where the sun rises. At this point in Daniel, the anti-Christ is destroying the nations of the southern alliance in the Middle East, far east from there would be Asia. The far east on the continent of Asia is China.

China is a nation with the world's largest standing army of 2 million strong and a population of almost 1.4 billion.

Many believe China will be America's next great enemy after Russia. The truth is China is the largest exporter to America, Over 18%. China's other exports go to America's ally Europe. To attack America at this time would be to destroy her economy.

China has an enemy in her backyard she must be watchful of. They fought in 1962, and today tensions are building again. She is a nation of over 1.3 billion people and is an American ally with nuclear capabilities. This is the nation of India.

Two enemies surround India. One is China, and the other is Pakistan, with a population of only 193 million and Nuclear capabilities. Unlike China and India, Pakistan is a Sunni Muslim nation. Rev 16:12 says Kings of the east. This means more than one. The other reference, believed to relate to the previous, is the Euphrates. Rev 9:14 speaks of a 200-million-man army. China and India individually are capable of such an army.

I speculate that when America's influence diminishes, Pakistan will strike India and will lose. A weakened India may join forces with China for the survival of their nations and attack the anti-Christ -or China and Pakistan may attack and defeat India.

RUSSIA

Dan 11:44 But tidings out of the east and out of **the north** shall trouble him:

126

The Hebrew word for north is "tsaphown," which means hidden, dark; used only of the north as a quarter (gloomy and unknown). This describes the Black and Caspian seas and mountain ranges of that area. Note: this is the king of the north concerned about the north. The only other countries north of Europe are Finland, Sweden, and Norway. They don't have the armies to challenge a significant threat and, to date, are part of Europe. Only one nation fits the criteria, Russia.

Russia is the largest nation by landmass in the world. The Russians have the second-largest army in the world. She has close to 4000 Aircraft, and her navy sports 352 vessels. She has 20,000 combat tanks and over 31,000 armored vehicles. Manpower is almost 800,000 active-duty personnel, with a national G.D.P. of about 1.3 trillion. Russia has the world's largest nuclear arsenal, estimated at over 7000.

The north is only mentioned in the final battle. This tells us Russia will not be destroyed in early battles. It is possible she will be diminished or maybe crippled. Looking at history, the mighty Magog has never been unseated from its place in the north.

After WWII under the Soviet Union, all religious institutions were torn down. The clergy were murdered or imprisoned. We're talking about a nation in that period, close to 170 million people. It's believed close to 60 million were murdered by their government. Today's population is only about 144 million.

When the cold war ended, and the Berlin wall came down in 1989, the Soviet Union collapsed, and Russia was reborn.

The Russian people began to experience the benefits of economic prosperity with a G.P.D. ranking 11th worldwide.

The government underwent reorganization. The Russian government spent over 100 million dollars building churches. Religion was restored, and great oppression lifted. Their people and lifestyles are very similar to most western nations. They love their children; Christianity influences their laws, and they don't want war.

Today Russia is extensively demonized by the West, especially the U.S. and Europe. The reason being she's an economic and military threat.

The unofficial spark that started both great world wars was Germany's fear of a Russian and French invasion, envying its strong economy. They struck first, both wars. For Russia to gain access to the European economy would shift the balance of power worldwide. Europe would have been defenseless against the Russian Bear after WWII. Therefore America stepped in. All the posturing we've seen in the last past century has been to prevent this.

Speculation: This is why I don't see the U.S. and Russia any time soon in **an all-out war,** or what many would see as the beginning of WWIII. Little would survive. I do see them in battle with one another in limited conflicts and over proxy countries. I don't believe the southern alliance can become strong when confronted with superpowers like Russia in their infancy.

CHAPTER 6

THE RISE OF THE BEAST/ A CHANGING WORLD

Interpreting tool

The rule of Inference. An inference is a fact reasonably implied from another fact. It is a logical consequence.

Jesus used this rule when he proved the resurrection of the dead in Matt. 22:23-33, by the scriptures, use of present tense, for a past event. Through this nugget, I discovered Egypt is not the king of the south but his partner. Inference is the detective work of scripture.

THE POWER BROKERS

Jesus said: Mat 6:24 No man can serve two masters: for either he will hate the one, and love the other; or else he will hold to the one, and despise the other. Ye cannot serve God and mammon.

One of the Great mysteries of the end times is found in Revelation Chapter Thirteen. It surrounds the mark of the beast. The Bible tells us the second beast (False Prophet) has control over world currency. Not just individuals but the entire economy of nations. How can nations be at war and yet submit under one financial institution? Remember, it's a loss at Cyprus that propels the anti-Christ to break the covenant. (Dan 11:30). After this come's the abomination that makes desolate and the mark. Why would all the nations agree to take this mark?

One major reason I'll cover later, but the other is a reality at work today that's often unseen. We focus on the mark, but the true point of the mark is allegiance and ownership. Throughout history and scripture, slaves and cattle were marked for ownership. The truth behind establishing the mark of the beast is a lust for power through finance. One of the greatest perversions of man's fallen nature is the use of power: to control, oppress, and enslave his fellow man. Jesus teaches the opposite to His disciples. He reveals the truly powerful use their advantage to love and serve.

Mark 10:42 But Jesus called them to Himself and said to them, "You know that those who are considered rulers over the Gentiles lord it over them, and their great ones exercise authority over them.:43 "Yet it shall not be so among you, but whoever desires to become great among you shall be your servant.:44 "And whoever of you desires to be first shall be slave of all.:45 "For even the Son of Man did not come to be served, but to serve, and to give His life a ransom for many."

The corruption that works through human pride pursues an image of superiority, seeks to amass power and control. The greater the control, the larger their perceived image becomes. Our perverse world seeks this through money.

One of the Devil's greatest apparatuses in the background of all the wars in the last days is the debt slavers, the hidden power broker, The Bankers.

These Bankers don't care about politics. When we look at colonialism or the destabilization of governments for business interest, in the background often unseen is the powerful banks that finance them. They often finance both sides and the business that controls them. If you study the last elections of the past two decades in the U.S., you will find the same powerful banking institutions had key members promoted to key posts in all the administrations. The men were chosen from banks that required bailouts and perpetrated fraud against the American people. As each President denounced the wickedness and corruption of Wall Street with one hand, they promoted representatives from each to key government positions with the other. They are concerned about the laws created that affect their enterprises. The influence of banks in politics is nothing new. Just follow the history of Private foreign banks in the United States.

Psa 94:20 Shall, the throne of iniquity, which devises evil by law, Have fellowship with You?:21 They gather together against the life of the righteous, And condemn innocent blood.

These Bankers are not concerned about wars, if it doesn't threaten their wellbeing. Wars are big business for banks, and they often finance both sides. The bank of England and the U.S. Federal Reserve financed Nazi Germany and the Allies. *Fort Russ News,5-14 2016.*

War means an increase in food, supplies, equipment, weapons, and lots of costs. Marine Brigadier General Smedley D. Butler, in his book, "War is a Racket," stated the average person does not understand what happens behind the scenes. He says, in WWI, a mere handful garnered the profits of conflicts. Twenty-one thousand new millionaires and billionaires were made in the war. None of them ever shoulder a rifle or dug a trench. These businesses went from peacetime to wartime with increases of 300, 500, and up to 900% profit. American Sugar Refining Company went from 200,000 a year to 6,000,000 a year during the war. Central Leather Company, before the war, averaged $1,167,000. During the war, they peaked at $15,500,000. Du Pont's average earning for the period 1910 to 1914 was six million dollars.

Their earnings from 1914 to 1918 reached fifty-eight million dollars, an increase of 950%. Stories like these can be repeated a hundred times.

Imagine your current yearly salary increases times five. Now imagine you live off that for four years, and then the money train stops. You go back to your regular salary. The profits from war can be very tempting to many. General Butler, in the back of his books, records the many gruesome pictures of WWI. One that is etched in my memory is a mountain of skulls. I find it interesting after one of the greatest wars ever fought in history, less than thirty years later, WWII began.

Hab 1:3 Why do You show me iniquity, And cause me to see trouble? For plundering and violence are before me; There is strife, and contention arises. :4 Therefore, the law is powerless, And justice never goes forth. For the wicked surround the righteous; Therefore perverse judgment proceeds.

These Bankers place little value on life. The Bible teaches the borrower is a slave to the lender. People are enslaved by debt. War places whole nations in debt. Great Brittan finally finished paying back its war loan from World War I in 2014. Banks also back the businesses that drive the war machine. Let's look at World War II. We saw businesses like Standard Oil supplied Hitler with Oil through Switzerland while he fought allied soldiers. They were adding aid to the bloodshed of their own country's youth. What a surprise to our troops to find the enemy soldiers were driving Fords and G.M Opel's. G.M. and Ford demanded compensation from the U.S. government after the war for damages to their German plants and received it! (Ref; Washington Post Staff Writer *By Michael Dobbs*, November 30, 1998)

These big businesses show how quickly human life is devalued when the opportunity for financial gain is presented. Standard Oil, partnering with German company I.G. Farben also supplied the key component for the gas used to exterminate millions of Jews in German concentration camps.

Innocent families are being tortured and destroyed while in the background, profiting from it all, the bankers.

The names of these banks can be deceiving because they are not owned nor controlled by the government but by private investors. President Abraham Lincoln faced this challenge during the civil war. Central bankers offered him a war loan with interest of over 30%. Lincoln declined. President Lincoln came up with the Greenback currency to finance the war and keep America out of the hands of European bankers. The Greenbacks printing was discontinued two years after his murder. President Andrew Jackson ran on the promise of destroying the power of the private banks in the United States. In 1832 Jackson ordered the withdrawal of government deposits from the Second Bank of America *(private central bank)* and instead had them put into safe banks. The Second Banks' head, Nicholas Biddle, openly threatened to cause a depression if the bank was not re-chartered. He called in existing loans and refusing to issue new loans, caused massive depression. In 1836 when the charter ran out, the Second Bank ceased to function. Andrew Jackson made two famous statements concerning the private banks: "The Bank is trying to kill me - but I will kill it!" and later, "If the American people only understood the rank injustice of our money and banking system - there would be a revolution before morning..."

Today central banks are found in almost every developed nation. Russia, China, Europe, Turkey, Saudi Arabia, and the list is exhaustive.

The only developing nations that don't operate on this system are Cuba, Iran, and North Korea. Central banks, private and public, adhere to government policies. Their status gives them special privileges smaller institutions don't have. A few of these are the ability to manipulate Interest rates and Federal Reserve bailout facilities. This means the people pay for their mistakes.

Large governments need a large purse to maintain their spending, especially for war. That's because government spending often exceeds revenue. They need powerful central banks.

Quote from former U.S. Representative Ron Paul: "The Purpose of a Central Bank Is to deceive and defraud the People."

The question today is who controls the central banks? The fed has twelve reserve banks districts throughout the U.S. They often go to great lengths to keep the methods of operation out of the public eye. The Federal Reserve has never been audited to the point that information is given on **how monetary policy is formed and its inner workings with foreign banks**. This information is off-limits to the fed's auditors as a matter of law passed in the 1970s. Yet this institution has great sway on America's financial future. (1978 Exclusions under the Federal Banking Agency Audit Act for the GAO audit)

Micah 2:1 Woe to them that devise iniquity, and work evil upon their beds! when the morning is light, they practice it because it is in the power of their hand.:2 And they covet fields, and take them by violence; and houses, and take them away: so they oppress a man and his house, even a man and his heritage.

The Bible tells us there will be a uniting of all central banks. (if it hasn't already happened) One great financial institution will govern the world economy in the Last Days. That institution will be controlled by the two nations of the false prophet. I find it interesting today that three of the world's most powerful financial institutions, The Federal Reserve, The World Bank, and The IMF, are headquartered in Washington D.C.

What these men don't realize is the God of mammon is a wicked taskmaster. They will find they're not in control but are being controlled by their lust. The sin that they serve will bring them into direct servitude to the serpent himself. The most horrific and terrible spirit will be made manifest to them, unleashing fears they could not Imagine. They will realize too late that the mark they've created is an irreversible curse of eternal damnation upon their souls.

James 5:1 Come now, you rich, weep and howl for your miseries that are coming upon you! 2 Your riches are corrupted, and your garments are moth-eaten. 3 Your gold and silver are corroded, and their corrosion will be a witness against you and will eat your flesh like fire. You have heaped up treasure in the last days.

THE BATTLES BEGIN / THE BEAST IS BORN

Neither the book of Daniel nor Revelation describes what battles take place during the beginning of sorrows, just the last week of years. **What we know** is what alliances they will make. The conflicts starting in the Middle East and worldwide will lead to one goal, the last day's alliances of the king of the South and the King of the North. It's a time of funneling and shaping for the last events. The King of the South-Turkey and his allies are Egypt, Ethiopia, Chub, Libya, the men of the league, and

Saudi Arabia. The king of the North- Europe and his allies are the false prophet (possibly America and Britain) and the Ten Kings. Even as I write this manuscript, transitions in the Middle East will lead to these alliances. There is a clear aligning of the southern alliance, and Turkey is slowly coming to the forefront. George Friedman: a U.S. geopolitical forecaster and strategist on international affairs, the author of the book The Next 100 years, has an uncanny ability to forecast changes on the international stage. His forecasts are so accurate some call his think tank the shadow CIA. He believes WWIII will be between Turkey and Poland. I find this interesting because this falls in line with the last day's scenario we see in scripture. While many E.U. nations have been flooded with Immigrants, Poland has kept its border closed and is thriving in nationalism and a booming economy. Poland has a strong Orthodox Catholic population.

The U.S. is also establishing strong ties to Poland. Poland may be the lead reformer of the E.U. nations.

We are about to see the birth pains intensify that Jesus spoke of in Mathew Chapter 24, with warfare that will shape the destiny of these nations. If you dig a little below the surface, you will see the motivation of these transitions is gain. They will seek to make a profit by selling arms. They will fight for assets and economic advantage. It's about national interest. The Bible also tells us **tribalism will play a major part**.

The nations surrounding the Mediterranean Sea have been the key to the rule of every major empire throughout history. These Middle Eastern conflicts will have a domino effect, eventually sparking other military confrontations on the world stage.

A new radical regime will emerge in Saudi Arabia with strong anti-west sentiments. The Turkish military will display its might. Their enemies will not stand before them. They will be seen as a deliverer in the eyes of the surrounding Sunni nations, and they will begin to rally behind them.

The king of the south will arise.

This will begin the rise of the Men of the League. A New Egyptian government embraces Sharia Law and enforces it. Ezekiel chapter 30 tells us before her destruction, Egypt prided in her strength, meaning she shall become a powerful nation in these times. Ethiopia and Chub align with their neighbor Egypt. They strengthen their ties to Egypt and Turkey.

Speculation: The Pro Sunni Muslim Brotherhood will retake the Egyptian government. Conflicts with Israel will begin with horrific consequences, yet she maintains her territories. Because of the Middle East proxy wars, the U.S. and Europe spin off into various confrontations. These battles don't lead to a full-blown world war, but that will be the rumor. The skirmishes will be devastating.

Speculation: America and Russia will reduce their military influence after these confrontations. America will fare better than her enemies, but her military will be greatly weakened. I believe she will then form a union with another nation of protestant heritage to compensate militarily and economically.

The European Union's inability to execute logistically will be an embarrassment. The lives lost due to the slowness of their bureaucracy will force massive changes in their government. (End of Speculation)

The King of the North arises as The Beast. A leader is given almost monarchal authority. He changes the entire structure of the E.U. and reformates the military into a powerful force. **The first king is the sign of this kingdom's beginning.** Up to this point, it has only been developing and transitioning.

What we see today is this prophecy arising from infancy. It's not the Beast of Revelation chapter 13, but like a moth from the cocoon, it will soon break forth. The beast will begin fighting for disputed territories and take them. The balance of world power will shift, and the beast will become the new world superpower. He will be demonically ruthless and seemingly unstoppable.

Speculation: The scripture clarifies that the antichrist was the king who recovered from the fatal wound in REV.13:14. This means he will be one of the first five rulers. I believe the anti-Christ will be the demonic <u>first and last</u> ruler, and he will receive his fatal wound in the beginning.

<u>THE DAYS OF DARKNESS</u>

John 9:4 I must work the works of him that sent me, while it is day: the night cometh, when no man can work.

It's important to understand that from the first king of the beast kingdom to the last will cover a period of about thirty-five to forty years. The current term limit in the E.U. is five years, and if they reduced it to four, it would be about twenty-eight to thirty-two years. I haven't calculated two-term leaders, which would increase this number if they have term limits. Remember Revelation Chapter 17 tells us there would be seven kings. We know Revelation 17 and Daniel 11 reveals the 6th king, the 7th with a partial rule, then the Anti-Christ. There are five administrations before them. We don't know which of the first five will be the Anti-Christ, the Devil's surrogate.

We know they will all be inspired by the dragon. We know this will be a very dark generation because the entire generation will worship the dragon.

The world will be in a state of constant conflict and war at this time. During this time, Christianity will be isolated and suppressed. To better illustrate, consider the last 3 ½ years of Daniel's 70th week. (Rev. 12:14-16) The 144,000 thousand will be Christ's witness to the world. Listen to a prophecy concerning them in Isa 66:19

(ICB) Isa 66:19 "I will put a mark on some of the people. And I will send some of these saved people to the nations. I will send them to Tarshish, Libya, Lud (the land of archers), Tubal, Greece, and all the faraway lands. **These people have never heard about what I have done. They have never seen my glory.** So the saved people will tell the nations about my glory.

Compared to Revelation Chpt. 7

Before the rapture or tribulation, they have silenced the truth of Christ. That will be the state of Christianity at this time. This is the night Jesus prophesied that "*No man can work.*"

Most agree the rapture of the church will happen before the final seven years or at least before the Great Tribulation. That leaves almost **thirty or more** years the Gospel message will be oppressed and eventually silenced and controlled. The church will go through this. Jesus tells us the decadence in this time will be like the days of Lot. He was vexed daily in public by their perverse deeds. Now is the time to speak! Now is the time to become strong!

During this time, the nation of Israel will be in confrontations and constant threats from her neighbors.

Amazingly enough, it will be the Nation of the Beast and False Prophet that keeps her enemies at bay. Daniel 11:15-22 makes clear there is an alliance there. For reparations, or another reason the Hebrew people will be allowed to build the temple on Mt Moriah; the place the Dome of the rock sits today.

During this time, Turkey will make a special covenant with Egypt and their allies and form a Middle East Alliance. The Men of the League will grow stronger. The Nations of the false prophet will become one. They will rename their nations and elect one leader. Consider the Persian and Meads.

The cruelty and conquest of the Beast nations will create great resentment from the king of the south.

Some action by the beast kicks off the retaliation we see in Daniel 11:7, where Turkey "deals with them."

THE REBUILDING OF THE TEMPLE

Israel, from the time of its rebirth, has been a place of miracles. One of the greater miracles happening today is often called the temple movement. The Key is Mt. Moriah. They built the temple outside of the city of David on the mountain.

Gen 22:1 And it came to pass after these things, that God did tempt Abraham, and said unto him, Abraham: and he said, Behold, here I am.:2 And he said, Take now thy son, thine only son Isaac, whom thou lovest, and get thee into the land of **Moriah**; and offer him there for a burnt offering upon one of **the mountains** which I will tell thee of.

2 Chr 3:1 Then Solomon began to build the house of the LORD at Jerusalem in **mount Moriah,**

where the Lord appeared unto David, his father, in the place that David had prepared in the threshing floor of Ornan the Jebusite.

Psa 48:1 A Song and Psalm for the sons of Korah. Great is the LORD, and greatly to be praised in the city of our God, in the **mountain** of his holiness.:2 Beautiful for situation, the joy of the whole earth, is mount Zion, on the sides of the north, the city of the great King.

All Holy and sacred sacrifices take place here, and this is where God instructed the temple to be built.

The only place on the planet where God says, "My Holy Mountain." Elevated overseeing His people on the northern side of Jerusalem, this is God's sacred Ground.

Ezek 43:12 This is the law of the house; Upon the top of the mountain the whole limit thereof round about shall be most holy. Behold, this is the law of the house.

Isa 56:7 Even them will I bring to my holy mountain, and make them joyful in my house of prayer: their burnt offerings and their sacrifices shall be accepted upon mine altar; for mine house shall be called an house of prayer for all people.

Mt. Moriah is where the Dome of the Rock is located. I have no idea how the Muslim landmark will be removed.

But it will. I can't tell you how the temple will be built. What I can declare is it will be rebuilt. The High Priest has been selected, the furniture and service utensils have been created. It seems all is in place, awaiting the time.

I believe before the seven-year period, the temple will be restored. In chapter 11, John is told to measure the Temple, Altar, and those worshiping there. There is a reason God brings this revelation of the temple to John.

Everything that happens after chapter three in the book of revelation is part of the final week.

What John measures will not change; the anti-Christ will defile the temple but not destroy it. The temple, the Altar, and God's people who worship there will be protected through the conflict. Daniel tells us:

Dan 11:32 And such as do wickedly against the covenant shall he corrupt by flatteries: but the people **that do know their God** shall be strong, and do exploits.

The Gentiles, John records, will trample the holy city. What he was instructed not to measure won't survive.

Speculation: The building of the temple will happen as a result of wars and conflicts in the Middle East. Concessions to the Hebrew people often come at the price of Jewish blood.

Daniel 9:27 Hints the Temple is built in accordance with the seven-year agreement, hinting it exists before the offerings begin. What we know for sure is the sacrificial offerings begin with it.

THE FINAL WEEK / THE LAST SEVEN YEARS

The 1st Strike Daniel 11:7

Dan 11:7 "But from a branch of her roots, one shall arise in his place, who shall come with an army, **enter the fortress of the king of the north, and deal with them and prevail.**

The 6th king of the nation of the beast makes a tragic mistake. He underestimates the resolve of the Middle East Alliances.

His decision causes a retaliatory strike from Turkey that devastates his army. We know it's retaliatory because he enters the Beast fortress, his strongest region, and withdraws. He made a point that can't be denied. There's a new sheriff in town.

There's a new superpower on the planet.

Dan 11:8 "And he shall also carry their gods captive to Egypt, with their princes and their precious articles of silver and gold; and he shall continue more years than the king of the north. Dan :9 So the king of the south shall come into his kingdom and shall return into his land.

Taking gods would make sense in our day and age. We know this is typical of radical Islam. It is the nature of radical Islamists to destroy the religious artifacts of the peoples they conquer. The Hebrew word for Princes in v8 is statues or images. They're taking Orthodox Christian art and treasures. They're plundering the churches and giving them to the nation of Egypt, possibly as first fruits. It's highly likely that Egypt, along the traditions of Islam, will burn them. It's possible what caused this event was directly related to the nation of Egypt. It's important to note that the King of Turkey will outlive the 6th king of the north.

Being the 7th king only lives a brief time, it's probable, this leader will also face the Anti-Christ. The Turkish forces return home.

Dan 11:10 But his sons shall be stirred up, and shall assemble a multitude of great forces: and one shall certainly come, and overflow, and pass through: then shall he return, and be stirred up, even to his fortress. :11 "And the king of the south shall be moved with rage, and go out and fight with him, with the king of the north, who shall muster a great multitude;

but the multitude shall be given into the hand of his enemy. :12 And when he hath taken away the multitude, his heart shall be lifted up; and he shall cast down many ten thousand: but he shall not be strengthened by it.

Some allayed states of the beast make an unauthorized attack on Turkey. The losses incurred in this battle set the Beast back years in his planned defeat of the Turkish alliance. These states will gather a substantial force, quickly pass through the Turkish border, and fight to the major Turkish defenses. Turkey, enraged, gathers their armies for battle. The Kingdom of the Beast supporting his allay comes with a larger force hoping to turn the battle into a northern win. The beast is gravely disappointed. The Turkish army shall be victorious. The victory will send the south into a warring frenzy on enemy territories when the battle is over.

They have just defeated the most powerful nation on the planet a second time. The word used for tens of thousands is the Hebrew word (:ribbow:H7239) used twice. (ribbon, ribbon) which means multitudes of thousands up to ten thousand times the same. The Turkish alliance will go on a fighting spree, slaughtering hundreds of thousands of their enemies.

Not just northern territories, I believe, Shiite territories and possibly Israeli as well. The scriptures say no advantage will be gained by it. They will still be unable to bring down the northern Beast kingdom. The beast will come back years later with a greater force and a more sophisticated arsenal.

Dan 11:14 And in those times there shall many stand up against the king of the south: also the robbers of thy people shall exalt themselves to establish the vision, but they shall fall.

144

The south will have many opponents over the next few years, possibly many radical, militant groups. The problem with pride is it's one-sided. Unnecessary carnage costs money, resources and makes enemies. The Bible notes a special group of radicals that attack the southern alliance from Israel. Their motivation is the "Vision." We aren't informed what the vision is, but Daniel knows and expects the reader to know. He calls it "the vision." They believe they can expedite God's prophecy concerning the Jewish people by stopping Turkey. The Southern alliance at this time could easily be mistaken for the beast. They fail and seemingly die in the attempt. What they do is so horrendous that the nation of Israel is charged with a war crime.

Dan 11:13 For the king of the north shall return, and shall set forth a multitude greater than the former, and shall certainly come after certain years with a great army and with much riches....:15 So the king of the north shall come, and cast up a mount, and take the most fenced cities: and the arms of the south shall not withstand, neither his chosen people, neither shall there be any strength to withstand.

When it comes to technology, a lot can change, especially in thirty years. The way wars were fought from WWI to WWII was night and day, and so was the equipment. We went from the 24lb black powder bombs drop by hand out of a fixed-wing aircraft to the Atomic Bomb, graduated from scout airplanes to attacking aircraft. WWII to Vietnam was the birth of the attack helicopter, jet planes, and guided missiles. Today we fight with unmanned vehicles, air, land, and sea. Computers and weapons from space are part of our arsenal. Most Americans don't even realize the U.S. Air force has a Space Wing. The weapons and method of warfare during the times of the beast are beyond my imagination. I have no doubt the nuclear bomb will be obsolete. We can only follow the narrative as close as possible.

The beast returns with force far greater than the previous. The technological advances facing the southern alliance on the field of battle are overwhelming. Turkey brings in the most elite fighters and most advanced resources. They are disadvantaged. The beast rises victorious.

Dan 11:16 But he that cometh against him shall do according to his own will, and none shall stand before him: and he shall stand in the glorious land, which by his hand shall be consumed. **:17** He shall also set his face to enter with the strength of his whole kingdom, and upright ones with him; thus shall he do: and he shall give him the daughter of women, corrupting her: but she shall not stand on his side, neither be for him.

This is when the beast looks to be invincible. With his alliance of the false prophet whose latest technology from space looks like fire from the heavens, the beast generates fear in his enemies. He begins his march into territories with little or no fight. The phrase "Glorious Land" is the same phrase used in v41 describing Israel. This means there's animosity between Europe and Israel, and other international nations. He marches into Israel, and the presence of his army consumes the city. Tactically he's set to invade the entire nation with another group called the upright ones. The Hebrew word means Just. (Possibly an armed force belonging to a world judicial group) A seemingly neutral Pro-tem leader is placed in charge of Israel called the Daughter of Women. (Possibly affiliated to the Upright ones) Unknown to the beast, she is pro-Israel or at least anti-beast.

Dan 11:18 After this shall he turn his face unto the isles, and shall take many: but a prince for his own behalf shall cause the reproach offered by him to cease; without his own reproach he shall cause it to turn upon him. :19 Then he shall turn his face toward the fort of his own land: but he shall stumble and fall, and not be found.

The sixth king of the beast begins a new campaign. His forces leave the Middle East, and the Bible says many nations fall. His conquest is interrupted. There seems to be an internal coup of some type, an attempt to stop his progress.

The word faces allude to the direction of his military. It's important to remember the beast is not some military general traveling with his army but the commander-in-chief calling shots from his capital. He turns his entire army toward his capital or base of operation, those abroad and at home. This would mean a massive conspiracy was unleashed against him. The beast is injured and dies in the confrontation. His body is never found.

The Seventh King.

Dan 11:20 Then shall stand up in his estate a raiser of taxes in the glory of the kingdom: but within few days he shall be destroyed, neither in anger nor in battle.

The word glory is a reference for Israel, specifically Jerusalem. The Seventh King of the North has Israel paying reparations. Why would you persecute a nation that attacked your enemy? Possibly the radicals used a weapon many nations had restrained from use at this point. Even nations locked in combat. Nevertheless, his term in office is cut short, and he dies seemingly by accident.

The Hebrew word for destroyed is "shabar." To be birth, be crushed, torn, or broken in some cases by mistake.

Dan 11:21 And in his estate shall stand up a vile person, to whom they shall not give the honor of the kingdom: but he shall come in peaceably, and obtain the kingdom by flatteries. **:22** And with the arms of a flood shall they be overflown from before him, and shall be broken; yea, also the prince of the covenant.

Revelation chapter 17 makes it clear. This is the Eighth and last king of this Northern Kingdom, the beast, the Anti-Christ, Satan's Surrogate for the last days. Daniel, receiving this vision, calls him the vile one. The world praises him, but the Jewish people see him with disdain and disgust. That's because he is very well known throughout Israel.

Speculation: They remember his first reign before his mortal wound. They remember the unnatural hatred in his eyes toward the Hebrew people. They remember the wickedness he rained down on them that caused this dishonoring. They have a history with this leader.

They don't show him the customary honors on his arrival. They hope under the leadership of the Daughter of Woman that the previous agreement made with the previous beast will hold. Being the snake he is, he disregards this and pulls another weapon from his demonic arsenal. Flattery: excessive and insincere praise, especially that given to further one's own interests. They give him what he requires. He later blows through their defenses as if they were nonexistent. He has broken the Israeli military and killed the prince of the covenant.

The word for covenant is the same word Daniel uses in chapter 9:27 for the seven-year agreement.

Dan 11:23 And after the league made with him he shall work deceitfully: for he shall come up, and shall **become strong** with a small **people.** **:24**

148

He shall enter peaceably even upon the fattest places of the province; and he shall do that which his fathers have not done, nor his fathers' fathers; he shall scatter **among them** the prey, and spoil, and riches: yea, and he shall forecast his devices against the strongholds, even for a time.

He will make an agreement with Israel. Daniel uses the word "chabar," which means to join sides or couple together. This is not the word Daniel uses for covenant in this chapter or chapter nine. This shows this is not the initial covenant spoken in chapter 9:27. He is offering Israel a special alliance. Israel agrees only to find out his word is worthless. The word "become" and "strong" are the same in Hebrew. Assam, which means: to crunch the bones: --break the bones.

The double use is to stress and emphasis the meaning. The word for "people" is Gentile. Shortly after the agreement is made, he sends in a small group of some of the most feared and fierce allies or generals. Gentile's whose reputation strikes fear for the cruelty of their deeds, butchers, and bone crushers. Violating the agreement, he invades and gives them the wealth of the land as a reward. Now the spirit of the Anti-Christ is truly revealed. He controls and plunders the wealth of Israel.

Dan 11:25 And he shall stir up his power and his courage against the king of the south with a great army; and the king of the south shall be stirred up to battle with a very great and mighty army; but he shall not stand: for they shall forecast devices against him. **:26** Yea, they that feed of the portion of his meat shall destroy him, and his army shall overflow: and many shall fall down slain. **:27** And both these kings hearts shall be to do mischief, and they shall speak lies at one table; but it shall not prosper: for yet the end shall be at the time appointed. **:28** Then shall he return into his land with great riches;

and his heart shall be against the holy covenant; and he shall do exploits, and return to his own land.

 The Anti-Christ moves his attention from Israel to the southern alliance.

The animosity between the South and North only grows. The Anti-Christ begins preparation for a campaign against Turkey. The Turks prepare for battle, gathering an enormous force from the allied nations, greatly increasing their odds for victory.

What the Turkish king doesn't expect is betrayal. Two trusted allied nations who were recipients of his support and aid turn on him in battle, the Libyans and the Ethiopians. Their treachery creates a vulnerability that causes the remaining forces to be overrun and many slaughtered by the Anti-Christ. The Anti-Christ gains significant wealth from this battle, but the tensions arising from the liberty of the Hebrews to worship at their temple annoy him. He is immersed in envy as he considers their commitment and sacrifices to their God. This does not flow with his vision of how things must be. He makes his disfavor known as he returns to the north.

Dan 11:29 At the time appointed he shall return, and come toward the south; but it shall not be as the former, or as the latter.:30 For the ships of Chittim shall come against him: therefore he shall be grieved, and return, and have indignation against the holy covenant: so shall he do; he shall even return, and have intelligence with them that forsake the holy covenant.

There's an ancient prophecy that predates Daniel. This may give us insight into why the Anti-Christ, losing the battle at Cypress, retaliates against Israel and why he commits the abomination in the temple. We find it in the prophecy of Balaam concerning the last days.

Num 24:23 And he took up his parable, and said, Alas, who shall live when God doeth this!:24 And ships shall come from the coast of Chittim, and shall afflict Asshur, and shall afflict Eber, and he also shall perish forever.

I could find no reference to ancient Ebers location and conflicting info on its people. Asshur in the time of Balaam is the Assyrian Empire which would comprise the corners of Syria, Iran, and Turkey and be centered in northern Iraq. What's amazing about this prophecy is we see another group today that wants to occupy and claim these same landmarks, Iraqi Kurdistan. The Kurds call it Southern Kurdistan, which would also comprise the corners of Syria, Iran, and Turkey and would be centered in northern Iraq. They've also been fighting for and are close to independents. Most of the Kurdish people are Sunni Muslim. Yet Kurds are an ethnic group more than a religious sect. This might explain why a Kurdish Jew serves as the Jewish representative of the Ministry of Endowment and Religious Affairs. Today their army stands at 250,000 troops but no navy. As we will discover, they have a special place in Bible prophecy.

This may be the reason, Balaam declares." who shall live when God doeth this! This prophecy was given before Israel became a nation. During this period, the Assyrian empire was land-locked. It had no navy! (est.1250 BC)

Its empire didn't expand to the coast until well after Israel became a nation. This prophecy has not taken place. Remember, this prophecy is about Jewish warships stopping Asshur.

Num 24:14 And now, behold, I go unto my people: come, therefore, and I will advertise thee what this people shall do to thy people in the latter days.

This people, refers to the children of Israel. Thy people are referring to something altogether different. Balak is from the tribe of Moab. He is not related to Asshur. He is a son of Lot, making him related to Israel. God was not speaking of Balak but his surrogate, the Devil. Balak wants to curse and destroy God's people, but he is unable because of the protective hand of God.

Balaam declares he saw Israeli ships destroying Asshur. This prophecy could mean the Kurds or mysterious Eber becomes a greater power in the region, and their influence will extend to the coast. In the next twenty to thirty years, these nations becoming a naval power is more than possible, especially if its ally is a superpower. Our text says they are part of the alliance of the kingdom of the beast.

If this prophecy holds for this time, we could see the rise of an independent Southern Kurdistan in league with the Beast and False Prophet.

The Anti-Christ begins his last campaign to destroy the Southern Alliance. As his massive navy nears Cypress, he suffers a surprise attack. Jewish radicals, possibly parts of the Israeli navy who stand for the vision, engage him. This unbelievable naval battle leaves no one standing.

The naval fleet of the beast is destroyed but so are their attackers. The beast is enraged. He now focuses on Israel. He will destroy the covenant. He gathers those sympathetic to his cause, that also hate the holy covenant, and they become the Anti-Christs' wedge. They give him the political edge he needs for the next step of his plan.

Speculation: They will accuse the Temple worship of being exclusive. The Anti-Christ will move in with his solution, give the world something he believes everyone could worship, himself.

MIDDLE OF THE WEEK / THE GREAT TRIBULATION

Dan 11:31 And arms shall stand on his part, and they shall pollute the sanctuary of strength, and shall take away the daily sacrifice, and they shall place the abomination that maketh desolate. :32 And such as do wickedly against the covenant shall he corrupt by flatteries: but the people that do know their God shall be strong and do exploits.:**33** And they that understand among the people shall instruct many: yet they shall fall by the sword, and by flame, by captivity, and by spoil, many days.

Now it begins. The beginning of the greatest time of persecution, anguish, and destruction the world has ever known. It all begins with the anti-Christ defiling what belongs to God, the Holy Temple.

Speculation: The bible emphasis the false prophet deceives by false signs and miracles. This could be the moment the Anti-Christ convinces the world he is the Messiah. It may even include explaining away the missing believers around the globe. In the Book of Revelation chapter 12, there is a depiction of the rapturing of the church in verses 10-12. This happens after a 3 ½ year period and is followed by another 3 ½ year period in v14. This could be his reasoning for attacking the covenant and a need for the false prophet's deception on a global scale. This may also explain a worldwide willingness to accept the mark of the beast. The disappearances have shaken the world, and there is a need for a unifying event. This might also explain why the battles seemed to stop, and the aggression turned towards believers.

(144,000 and those refusing the mark) It's only near the end of the last 3 ½ years that we see conflicts stir among nations.

I believe the judgments released in the great tribulation are so catastrophic; wars won't be possible. The world will be thrown into economic, environmental, and ecological chaos. (End of speculation)

The false prophet, through great deception, calls for the creation of an image in the likeness of the beast. Revelation chapter 13 tells us that the world participates in its creation, not just a copy of his physique but also an infusion of his consciousness. The words "give life" mean to give it a soul. They give it an artificial mind that mimics his emotional responses and thinking. This is a monument to his glory, the glory of his perceived resurrection testimony. They build a throne and place it into the holy place. Then the android-like copy of the Anti-Christ takes his seat among the holy furniture and the holy of holies as if all its symbolism points to him as God... And he causes all, both small and great, rich and poor, free and bond, to receive a mark in their right hand or their foreheads. I believe this will be the pledge of devotion. By doing this, they make this image their provider, the provider of all mankind. Those who will not obey will starve and die by beheading. Those nations that will not comply will be destroyed.

(Rev 13:14-15)

Chaos breaks loose in Jerusalem. The military of the beast overpowers all Israeli resistance as Jewish people are divided on what course to take.

Some traitorous leaders within the Jewish community sell out the People of God for gain. Those that realize what's happening try to stand. They spread the truth, and many hear their instruction, but the worldliness of others blinds them to the truth.

154

These great saints who try to resist will be weakened but will be helped and aided in this dark time. Many will join them that are not committed simply out of fear. For many days, they resist, but eventually, they're hunted down in their homes, streets, and businesses; for a final opportunity to pledge their loyalty to the beast. The disloyal are beheaded. Some will even be burned alive as public spectacles or just imprisoned until execution. They will be martyrs for the cause and become examples of faithfulness to those that are left.

Around the world, the worshippers of the beast say, "Who is like the beast? Who can make war with him?" And for the next 3 1\2 years, the beast and his copy will speak blasphemies and exalt themselves as gods. The wickedness of his immoral nature will come out along with his hatred of women, lust for power, and strength. He will declare himself the God of gods, yet he will honor the Gods of strength and power. Those who pursue this he will honor and divide the spoils of the land. (Rev 13:4-5) (Dan 11:35-39)

2 Th 2:3 Let no man deceive you by any means: for that day shall not come, except there come a falling away first, and that man of sin be revealed, the son of perdition:4 Who opposeth and exalteth himself above all that is called God, or that is worshipped; so that he as God sitteth in the temple of God, showing himself that he is God.

Mat 24:15 When ye therefore shall see the abomination of desolation, spoken of by Daniel the prophet, stand in the holy place, (whoso readeth, let him understand:)

IT IS TIME TO RUN!

God warns wherever you are when this happens, immediately find a place of refuge.

Look above or underground because the forces of evil will be coming for you. They will be seeking your pledge to the beast. Hear the urgency of Christ's warning to this generation.

Mat 24:16 Then let them which be in Judaea flee into the mountains:17 Let him which is on the housetop not come down to take anything out of his house:18 Neither let him which is in the field return to take his clothes.19 And woe unto them that are with child, and to them that give suck in those days!:20 But pray ye that your flight be not in the winter, neither on the sabbath day:

The entire cashless financial system of the whole world will be on lockdown.

Law enforcement will have already been preparing for this announcement and will systematically track and apprehend dissidents. We can only imagine the technology 30 or more years from now.

Dan 7:25 And he shall speak great words against the most High, and shall wear out the saints of the Most High, and think to change times and laws: and they shall be given into his hand until a time and times and the dividing of time.

The Bible tells us the Jewish Evangelist; the 144,000 will flee Israel and begin their mission to the world, taking the gospel to those who are lost. The armies of the Anti-Christ's pursuit of them will fail. (Rev 12:14-17) They warn all clearly of the eternal consequences in this time...

Rev 14:9 And the third angel followed them, saying with a loud voice, If any man worship the beast and his image, and receive his mark in his forehead, or in his hand,:10 The same shall drink of the wine of the wrath of God, which is poured out without mixture into the cup of his indignation;

and he shall be tormented with fire and brimstone in the presence of the holy angels, and in the presence of the Lamb::11 And the smoke of their torment ascendeth up forever and ever: and they have no rest day nor night, who worship the beast and his image, and whosoever receiveth the mark of his name.

At this time, two prophets rise up, and the Great Tribulation will begin! God makes clear what brings this disaster. He taught this lesson to His people in Ezek 5:11-12...

...'Therefore, as I live,' says the Lord GOD, 'surely, **because you have defiled My sanctuary** with all your detestable things and with all your abominations, therefore I will also diminish you; My eye will not spare, nor will I have any pity. 12 'One-third of you shall die of the pestilence, and be consumed with famine in your midst; and one-third shall fall by the sword all around you; and I will scatter another third to all the winds, and I will draw out a sword after them.

The Day of Christ has begun. What's spoken in heaven will be worked through these prophets on earth. They will have a supernatural ministry out of Jerusalem by which they cannot be killed by any means for 3 ½ years.

The media will be glued to every word they say, and the world will hate them. (Rev 11:6)

Rev 11:5 And if anyone wants to harm them, fire proceeds from their mouth and devours their enemies. And if anyone wants to harm them, he must be killed in this manner.:6 These have power to shut heaven, so that no rain falls in the days of their prophecy; and they have power over waters to turn them to blood, and to strike the earth with all plagues, as often as they desire.:7 When they finish their testimony, the beast that ascends out of the bottomless pit will make war against them, overcome them, and kill them.:8 And their dead bodies will lie in the street of the great city which spiritually is called Sodom and Egypt, where also our Lord was crucified.

The next several years after the abomination will be a time of purging. Instead of global war, there will be a war against the saints. The 144,000 will be remarkably successful in getting their message to a lost world. John records this concerning them:

Rev 7:9 After this I beheld, and, lo, a great multitude, which <u>no man could number</u>, of all nations, and kindreds, and people, and tongues, stood before the throne, and before the Lamb, clothed with white robes, and palms in their hands;

Many will stand up and recognize the true and living God. The God of love and mercy and freedom versus the man of pride and wrath. But the price for this decision will be great.

Rev 20:4 And I saw thrones, and they sat upon them, and judgment was given unto them: and I saw the souls of them <u>that were beheaded for the witness of Jesus</u>, and for the word of God, and which had not worshipped the beast, neither his image, neither had received his mark upon their foreheads or in their hands; and they lived and reigned with Christ a thousand years.

The book of revelation is not focused primarily on the wars but God's judgments upon the nation by natural, supernatural, and human agents. We have hints of a few. The devastation in this time will be unparalleled. People will be scrambling to survive.

1/5 of all the trees and grass on the planet will be burnt by meteor storms. An asteroid somehow sets off a chain reaction destroying our freshwater sources, rivers, and lakes, starting with a third of the planet. Some type of weapon is launched into one of the oceans, creating a tsunami so large the bible records 1/3 of the ships are destroyed. (Rev 8:8)

Can you imagine the coastal damage and loss of life? There will be mass spreading of disease and famine. The heat from the sun will be so fierce that daily activities will cease, and people will only venture out at night. These are only a few mentioned calamities throughout the book of Revelation.

Then near the end of the final week, the two prophets are killed. The two martyred witnesses lay dead and discarded in the streets of Jerusalem. It has been three and a half days since their murder. Symbolic of the three and a half years, the temple has been dead through its defilement. The world has made this a time of rejoicing and gift-giving, shaking their fist in the face of the Almighty.

In the face of these great signs and wonders, they will not turn from the wickedness of their ways. They refuse to repent!

The prophets stand to their feet, and the world stops. Yes, these dead men rise to their feet. Every station, every news outlet, every source of communications broadcast as the world stares in horror. They're alive! The reality of life after death, the truth about the resurrection and eternal damnation, all the truth they resisted and sought to hide stands before them in the glory of the one who has power over death and life, hell and the grave. Then a voice calls out from heaven, "come up here."

Their bodies begin to levitate. Gravity can't hold them. The cameras pan upward as the bodies disappear into the sky. The time has come! (Rev.11v9-12)

THE LAST CAMPAIGN /ARMAGEDDON

Dan 11:40 "*At the time of the end the king of the south shall attack him; and the king of the north shall come against him like a whirlwind, with chariots, horsemen, and with many ships; and he shall enter the countries, overwhelm them, and pass through.*

The king of the south will not bow! If the southern alliance accepted the mark, the Lordship of the beast, why are they revolting?

I don't believe this attack had anything to do with the mark. The beast had power over the south while implementing the mark. Several years have passed, and they have regrouped. They're not buying into his Lordship. Their earlier resistance would have been met with slaughter. What this tells us is the mark doesn't control mankind's decisions. It just guarantees a seat in hell. The reason for the battle is found here...

Rev 16:13 And I saw three unclean spirits like frogs come out of the mouth of <u>the dragon</u>, and out of the mouth of <u>the beast</u>, and out of the mouth of <u>the false prophet</u>. :14 For they are the spirits of devils, working miracles, which go forth unto the kings of the earth and of the whole world, to gather them <u>to the battle of that great day of God Almighty</u>.:15 Behold, I come as a thief. Blessed is he that watcheth, and keepeth his garments, lest he walk naked, and they see his shame.:16 And he gathered them together into a place called in the Hebrew tongue Armageddon.

This is preparation for the final conflict, The Day of the Lord. All nations verge on Jerusalem for this final conflict.

Taking the first strike doesn't benefit the Southern alliances. The Beast alliance rolls through the south like a freight train. Then all-out war! He begins his rampage through all the Middle East alliances of the south, and the word the Bible uses is "overwhelm." NKJV

Dan 11:41 He shall enter also into the glorious land, and many countries shall be overthrown: but these shall escape out of his hand, even Edom, and Moab, and the chief of the children of Ammon.

Israel doesn't escape. This prophetic Psalms describes what is to come.

Psa 79:1 A Psalm of Asaph. O God, the heathen are come into thine inheritance; thy holy temple have they defiled; they have laid Jerusalem on heaps.:2 The dead bodies of thy servants have they given to be meat unto the fowls of the heaven, the flesh of thy saints unto the beasts of the earth.:3 Their blood have they shed like water round about Jerusalem; and there was none to bury them.

All the nations surrounding Israel suffer his wrath with an unusual exception, Edom, Moab, and Ammon. The word escape means released as in to be freed. These are the ancient traditional enemies of Israel, and they shall be spared. Many nations fall at this point. Egypt will also be the focus of God's wrath.

BABYLONS FALL

The Ten Kings have received their kingdoms. They fight alongside the armies of the beast. Their first order of business is the destruction of the harlot.

The religious, hypocritical whore that hindered their secular ambitions must be destroyed. Ten nations will descend on the city in one day and utterly wipe it from the face of the planet. Of all the colors we hear the harlot wears, the linen, scarlet, the purple, gold, silver, and various jewels, we never hear of the blue. Blue is symbolic of God's word. (Num 15:38-50)

Rev 17:16 "And the ten horns which you saw on the beast, these will hate the harlot, make her desolate and naked, eat her flesh and burn her with fire.:17 "For God has put it into their hearts to fulfill His purpose, to be of one mind, and to give their kingdom to the beast until the words of God are fulfilled.

Rev 18:2 And he cried mightily with a loud voice, saying, "Babylon the great is fallen, is fallen, and has become a dwelling place of demons, a prison for every foul spirit, and a cage for every unclean and hated bird! **Rev 18:7-17**

EGYPT'S FALL

Dan 11:42 He shall stretch forth his hand also upon the countries: and the land of Egypt shall not escape... **Dan 11:43** But he shall have power over the treasures of gold and of silver, and overall the precious things of Egypt: and the Libyans and the Ethiopians shall be at his steps.

Egypt is in a struggle of her own. **Ezek 30:4** And the sword shall come upon Egypt, and great pain shall be in Ethiopia when the slain shall fall in Egypt, and they shall take away her multitude, and her foundations shall be broken down.

The word slain is Hebrew word "chalal," (*pierced to death); fig. polluted:--kill, profane, slain.*) The armies and allies of the anti-Christ are eradicating the forces of Egypt. Troops from western Turkey (Lydia) come to her aid along with the standing troops of Chub; multiple battles throughout Egypt with the mingled people and the men of the league all fall. No one that allied with Egypt will survive, and then God promises Egypt will burn. Dan 11:42 (speaking of the anti-Christ)

He shall stretch forth his hand also upon the countries: and the land of Egypt shall not escape. The traitors of Egypt, Libya, and Ethiopia will follow him.

Ezekiel Chapter 30 shows us the Judgment of Ethiopia, and by proxy Libya, is not with Egypt. It comes at the hand of someone other than the Anti-Christ in a battle that follows.

Ezek 30:9 In that day shall messengers go forth from me in ships to make the careless Ethiopians afraid, and great pain shall come upon them, as in the day of Egypt: for, lo, it cometh

RUSSIA AND CHINA DRAWN TO BATTLE

Dan 11:44 But tidings out of the east and out of the north shall trouble him: therefore he shall go forth with great fury to destroy, and utterly to make away many. :45 And he shall plant the... ...tabernacles of his palace between the seas in the glorious holy mountain; yet he shall come to his end, and none shall help him.

Marching from the east is an army of two hundred million. From the far north marches another army, not as large but of substantial size and power. He unleashes the full power of his armies with his alliances on those opposing nations left in the region and prepares his last stand from Israel. The Scriptures best describes what comes next. These are all scriptures about the day of the Lord; some will be from the book of Revelation.

1 Th 5:2 For yourselves know perfectly that **the day of the Lord so cometh as a thief in the night.**:3 For when they shall say, Peace and safety; then sudden destruction cometh upon them, as travail upon a woman with child; **and they shall not escape.** ^{Joel 2:1} Blow ye the trumpet in Zion, and sound an alarm in my holy mountain:

let all the inhabitants of the land tremble: for the day of the LORD cometh, for it is nigh at hand; 2 A day of darkness and of gloominess, a day of clouds and of thick darkness, as the morning spread upon the mountains: **a great people and a strong; there hath not been ever the like, neither shall be any more after it, even to the years of many generations.** ^{Joel 2:31} The sun shall be turned into darkness, and the moon into blood, before the great and the terrible day of the LORD come. ^{Joel 3:14} **Multitudes, multitudes in the valley of decision:**

For the day of the LORD is near in the valley of decision. ^{Zec 14:1} Behold, the day of the LORD cometh, and thy spoil shall be divided in the midst of thee.:2 **For I will gather all nations against Jerusalem to battle**; and the city shall be taken, and the houses rifled, and the women ravished, and half of the city shall go forth into captivity, and the residue of the people shall not be cut off from the city

Isa 2:12 For the day of the LORD of hosts shall be upon **every one that is proud and lofty, and upon every one that is lifted up; and he shall be brought low:**

Isa 13:9 Behold, the day of the LORD cometh, cruel both **with wrath and fierce anger, to lay the land desolate: and he shall destroy the sinners** thereof out of it.:10 For the stars of heaven and the constellations thereof shall not give their light: the sun shall be darkened in his going forth, and the moon shall not cause her light to shine.11 **And I will punish the world for their evil**, and the wicked for their iniquity; **and I will cause the arrogancy of the proud to cease** and will lay low the haughtiness of the terrible.**12 I will make a man more precious than fine gold**; even a man than the golden wedge of Ophir. ^{Zep 1:14} The great day of the LORD is near, it is near, and hasteth greatly, even the voice of the day of the LORD:

the mighty man shall cry there bitterly.:15 That day is **a day of wrath, a day of trouble and distress**, **a day of wasteness and desolation, a day of darkness and gloominess, a day of clouds and thick darkness,:16 A day of the trumpet and alarm** against the fenced cities, and against the high towers.

THE SECOND COMING

Rev 19:11-15 And I saw heaven opened, and behold a white...horse; and he that sat upon him was called Faithful and True, and in righteousness, he doth judge and make war. His eyes were as a flame of fire, and on his head were many crowns; and he had a name written, that no man knew, but he himself. And he was clothed with a vesture dipped in blood: and his name is called The Word of God. And the armies which were in heaven followed him upon white horses, clothed in fine linen, white and clean. And out of his mouth goeth a sharp sword, that with it he should smite the nations: and he shall rule them with a rod of iron: and he treadeth the winepress of the fierceness and wrath of Almighty God.

Rev 17:13 These have one mind, and shall give their power and strength unto the beast.:14 These shall make war with the

Lamb, and the Lamb shall overcome them: for he is Lord of lords, and king of kings: and they that are with him are called, and chosen, and faithful. ^{Zec.14:3} **Then shall the LORD go forth, and fight against those nations**, as when he fought in the day of battle.:4 And **his feet shall stand in that day upon the Mount of Olives**, which is before Jerusalem on the east, and **the mount of Olives shall cleave in the midst thereof toward the east and toward the west, and there shall be a very great valley;** and half of the mountain shall remove toward the north, and half of it toward the south. ^{Joel 3:15} The sun and the moon shall be darkened, and the stars shall withdraw their shining. 16 **The LORD also shall roar out of Zion, and utter his voice from Jerusalem; and the heavens and the earth shall shake: but the LORD will be the hope of his people**, and the strength of the children of Israel.

Zep 1:17 And **I will bring distress upon men, that they shall walk like blind men**, because they have sinned against the LORD: and **their blood shall be poured out as dust, and their flesh as the dung.** ^{Rev 14:20 NRSV} **And the winepress was trodden outside the city, and blood flowed from the winepress, as high as a horse's bridle, for a distance of about two hundred miles**. ^{Rev 11:18} And **the nations were angry, and thy wrath is come,** and the time of the dead, that they should be judged, and that thou shouldest give reward unto thy servants the prophets, and to the saints, and them that fear thy name, small and great; **and shouldest destroy them which destroy the earth.** ^{Rev 19:20} **And the beast was taken, and with him the false prophet** that wrought miracles before him, with which he deceived them that had received the mark of the beast, and them that worshipped his image. **These both were cast alive into a lake of fire** burning with brimstone. ^{Isa 13:13} Therefore **I will shake the heavens, and the earth shall remove out of her place,** in the wrath of the LORD of hosts, and in the day of his fierce anger. **2 Pet 3:10** But the day of the Lord will come as a thief in the night; in **the which the heavens shall pass away with a great noise, and the elements shall melt with fervent heat, the earth also and the works that are therein shall be burned up** .... IT IS FINISHED.

45 DAYS

The scripture tells us the earth will be purged. Peters says the elements melt. The last judgment on the earth is fire. Many believe this will result from a large asteroid striking the earth. The massive debris after impact flaying out into the atmosphere and then reentering will catch fire, creating an oven effect that would burn and set fire on everything on the planet. The angel encourages Daniel in chapter 12.

Dan 12:11 "And from the time that the daily sacrifice is taken away, and the abomination of desolation is set up, there shall be one thousand two hundred and ninety days. :12 "Blessed is he who waits, and comes to the one thousand three hundred and thirty-five days.

This catastrophic event won't ruin the planet for a hundred years or make the earth uninhabitable, as most science predicts for an event like this. God says, in forty-five days, mankind can surface. They must wait exactly forty-five days. Humanity can begin again. I estimate that the number that survives will be less than 15% of the earth's original population. All the deadly residue of weapons used and contaminates that polluted the planet will be purged. This will be the ultimate burnt offering. There will be no factories, banks, or industry; no buildings at all.

167

The only surviving structure will be the temple, which is supernaturally preserved. The fresh, beautiful seedlings of plant life will spring forth as nature surfaces from hiding. Man will start again like in the Garden of Eden led by Christ.

Isa 2:2 And it shall come to pass in the last days, that the mountain of the Lord's house shall be established in the top of the mountains, and shall be exalted above the hills; and all nations shall flow unto it.:3 And many people shall go and say, Come ye, and let us go up to the mountain of the LORD, to the house of the God of Jacob; and he will teach us of his ways, and we will walk in his paths: for out of Zion shall go forth the law, and the word of the LORD from Jerusalem.:4 And he shall judge among the nations, and shall rebuke many people: and they shall beat their swords into plowshares, and their spears into pruninghooks: nation shall not lift up sword against nation, neither shall they learn war any more.

Interpreting tool

Precedent. Confirmation of truth. A common phrase in the New Testament is "This is that." *Acts 2:16 But <u>this is that</u> which was spoken by the prophet Joel.* The subject Peter spoke on has numerous accounts in scripture. It's important to find what common denominator ties an event or season together. **Can you prove a pattern in scripture? Does it flow within a book or Testament or both Testaments**? Example: Shed blood is symbolic of the sacrifice of life.

We find a pattern of truth that flows from one Testament to another. This is key in prophecy. In this book, I distinguished Millennial prophesies from tribulation prophesies by a phrase pattern used throughout the Bible.

CHAPTER 7

A THOUSAND YEARS OF CHANGE

The only war to cover at the end of the Millennial would be the battle with Gog of Magog, which we have covered pretty well. I believe it's important to cover certain destinies of the Millennial Kingdom that help understand truths we may not touch upon otherwise. I'm speaking of the differences between the New Heaven and Earth versus the millennial kingdom. First, let's look at the millennial reign of Christ.

THE THOUSAND-YEAR REIGN (Millennium)

(versus) NEW HEAVEN AND EARTH

Rev 20:2 And he laid hold on the dragon, that old serpent, which is the Devil, and Satan, and bound him a thousand years, ...Rev 20: 5 But the rest of the dead lived not again until the thousand years were finished. This is the first resurrection.:6 Blessed and holy is he that hath part in the first resurrection: on such the second death hath no power, but they shall be priests of God and of Christ, and shall reign with him a thousand years.:7 And when the thousand years are expired, Satan shall be loosed out of his prison,

The Thousand-Year Reign is a time of perfect peace and governance under Christ. The proclamation at the end of the tribulation is the kingdoms of this world are now the kingdoms of our God! The world will become an Eden where all the sons of Adam can experience life in fellowship with God, unhindered by the serpent.

Love towards one another can genuinely flourish as we rebuild our world under God's guidance.

Revelations Chpt.20 shows us the perfect order. After the judgment of the world's armies by our Lord, the Devil is bound for the duration of the millennium. The tribulation saints will reign with Christ during this period, as will all who are part of the first resurrection. (See also 2 Tim 2:12) How we will reign is a bit of a mystery. We know those that have been resurrected will have glorified bodies and dwell and conduct business among those that are human. The tribulation Martyrs will serve in the temple. (Rev 7:14-15) All who were resurrected before the tribulation will Judge the Gentile World. (1Cor 6:2) The Apostles will Judge the Jewish people. (Luke 22:29) The 144,000 will be priests and Levites to God. (Isa.66:19-22)

There will also be a remarkable quality of life. People will live longer. Individuals who reach the age of a hundred will physically be as a child. There will be a harmony in nature that hadn't existed since the Garden of Eden; the lion will lie down with the lamb.

There is also a period of unknown time. Satan is loosed after the millennium. There is no time given for when nations are corrupted and rebel under the leadership of Gog of Magog. They are eradicated, and then comes the time of the Great White Throne Judgment. We are not privy to how long this takes. We know that after this, the influence of evil is finally disposed of.

THE NEW HEAVEN AND EARTH.

There can be confusion about the placement of the New Heaven and Earth in prophecy. Some believe it follows the tribulation's end. Others think it's at the millennium's end. Others confuse the two as one. Note these two accounts:

Isa 65:17-25 For, behold, I create new heavens and a new earth: and the former shall not be remembered, nor come into mind.:18 But be ye glad and rejoice forever in that which I create: for, behold, I create Jerusalem a rejoicing, and her people a joy.:19 And I will rejoice in Jerusalem, and joy in my people: and the voice of weeping shall be no more heard in her, nor the voice of crying.:20 There shall be no more thence an infant of days, nor an old man that hath not filled his days: for the child shall die an hundred years old; but the sinner being an hundred years old shall be accursed.:21 And they shall build houses, and inhabit them; and they shall plant vineyards, and eat the fruit of them.:22 They shall not build, and another inhabit; they shall not plant, and another eat: for as the days of a tree are the days of my people, and mine elect shall long enjoy the work of their hands.:23 They shall not labour in vain, nor bring forth for trouble; for they are the seed of the blessed of the LORD, and their offspring with them.:24 And it shall come to pass, that before they call, I will answer; and while they are yet speaking, I will hear.:25 The wolf and the lamb shall feed together, and the lion shall eat straw like the bullock: and dust shall be the serpent's meat. They shall not hurt nor destroy in all my holy mountain, saith the LORD.

Rev 20:15 And whosoever was not found written in the book of life was cast into the lake of fire. Rev 21:1 And I saw a new heaven and a new earth: for the first heaven and the first earth were passed away; and there was no more sea.

:2 And I John saw the holy city, new Jerusalem, coming down from God out of heaven, prepared as a bride adorned for her husband.:3 And I heard a great voice out of heaven saying, Behold, the tabernacle of God is with men, and he will dwell with them, and they shall be his people, and God himself shall be with them, and be their God.:4 And God shall wipe away all tears from their eyes; and there shall be no more death, neither sorrow, nor crying, neither shall there be any more pain: for the former things are passed away.

At first glance, there might seem to be some contradictions, but you will see they cover different issues with a closer look. First, it's essential to notice these scriptures speak of a New Heaven and Earth and Jerusalem. The prophecies concerning Jerusalem are not the same. Rev.21 says a New Jerusalem will come down from heaven. The account in Isaiah speaks of a Jerusalem on earth.

The subject of a New Heaven and Earth ends in the same verse in Isaiah 65v17, and the remaining eight verses speak about earthly Jerusalem and the joy God will make it. In this Jerusalem, death still reigns, not so in Rev. Chapter 21. The Isaiah 65 account is the Jerusalem of the millennium kingdom. The account in Revelation is the crown of the New Heaven and Earth when the millennium ends.

NEW DESTINIES FOR EGYPT AND ASSYRIA

This is why we don't find Egypt in the Ezekiel 38 prophecies. Those prophecies concern the end of the millennium.

Egypt is part of the kingdom of God and not its adversaries at this time. Egypt holds a special place in scripture. It's one of the most recognizable nations in the Bible, mentioned over 611 times, second only to the nation of Israel. We often see Egypt in its darkest moments.

Deu 8:14 Then thine heart be lifted up, and thou forget the LORD thy God, which brought thee forth out of the land of Egypt, from the house of bondage;

The enslavement of the Hebrew people and the genocide committed to destroying their deliverer.

Many of Egypt's mentions in the scripture are for this very purpose, the analogy of leaving the old life and crossing over the Red Sea to a new beginning.

There was much more to Egypt. It was a place of refuge for Abraham in a time of famine. It became a refuge for nations in the time of Joseph's famine. It became a refuge for our Lord from a murderous king. It's important to remember the redemptive power of God toward humanity. In Egypt, we see how God turns the house of bondage into a refuge of hope.

Please hear this powerful prophecy of the Second Coming of Christ Isa 19:1...

The burden of Egypt. Behold, the LORD rideth upon a swift cloud, and shall come into Egypt: and the idols of Egypt shall be moved at his presence, and the heart of Egypt shall melt in the midst of it.

Isa 19:22 And the LORD shall smite Egypt: he shall smite and heal it: and they shall return even to the LORD, and he shall be entreated of them, and shall heal them.:23 In that day shall there be a highway out of Egypt to Assyria, and the Assyrian shall come into Egypt, and the Egyptian into Assyria, and the Egyptians shall serve with the Assyrians.:24 In that day shall Israel be the third with Egypt and with Assyria, even a blessing in the midst of the land.

We often see Israel as the light to the world in the 1000 year reign. God says they are only a third of the equation. God says in ...Isa 19:25 Whom the LORD of hosts shall bless, saying, Blessed be Egypt my people, and Assyria the work of my hands, and Israel mine inheritance.

For God, this is personal." Assyria is the work of my hand." God says he has been at work in the molding of this nation. These are the Kurds of Southern Kurdistan, the descendants of the ancient nation of the Medes. God will redeem a nation from every significant player in these conflicts to play a particular part in humanity's restoration.

He says Egypt My People. This is a mystery I hope to discover at another date. How wondrous are the mercies of God! The enemies of His inheritance share in the glory of His Kingdom.

We saw the Coptic believers being crucified on trees during the Arab Spring. What we witnessed was the enemy shaking his fist in defiance of the destiny of a nation. This is rebellion at its worst, just like the proverbial Paul the Apostle kicking against the pricks. The God of all mercy shall humble them, break them, and save them. There is hope for the worst in humanity. Keep praying.

My goal and hope is that you are challenged to search the scriptures in the Bible, even if you disagree with my conclusions. The church needs more than ever men and women who are strong in the word and the power of his might. If you're a minister, I hope you found some sermon material. May God use and bless you,

Virgil L Thomas

Other References: King James Version, New King James Version

The Middle East: Thomas G Kavunedus & Harold Hammond Globe Books ISBN 087065635x

How Islam Plans to Change the World: William Wagner Kregel Publishing ISBN 978082543929-2

Explore the book: J Sidlow Baxter. Academic Book 1415 Luke drive S.E. Grad Rupidge Michigan 49506 L C C C N 60 – 50187

Foundations of Pentecostal Theology L.I. F.E. Bible College at Los Angeles L C C C N Box 8762 Zip Code 5084

ABINGDON'S STRONG'S EXHAUSTIVE CONCORDANCE L C C C N BS 425.58. copyright 1980

Things To Come. J Dewright Pentecost Copyright 1958 1SBN 0-310 30890-9 Zondervan

Ancient History Encyclopedia /online

Other books by the author.

THE TIMES

WISDOM FROM JOB

CHURCH QUAKES

PRECEPT UPON PRECEPT

Made in the USA
Columbia, SC
24 June 2023

18833923R00098